Praise for
Net, Blogs and Rock 'n' Roll

"This is a really important book. David Jennings has done a great job shedding light on all sorts of issues and the pyramids of influence is a fantastic way of talking about the music consumer space. Net Blogs and Rock 'n' Roll has changed the way I think about targeting consumers. It is a super read and should be on the shelf of everyone who cares about how people find new music and media that matches their tastes."
Paul Lamere, Sun Microsystems

"David Jennings is the Christopher Columbus of digital discovery, and his pioneering book is an extremely helpful map of the complex new world of online music. Equally relevant for consumers and artists, this is the first book that gets beyond the rhetoric and professionally charts the cartography of the digital revolution."
Andrew Keen, founder of Audiocafe.com and author of
The Cult of the Amateur

"The internet is leading to dramatic changes in the media industry. Fans and industry professionals will appreciate how *Net, Blogs and Rock 'n' Roll* gets beyond the rhetoric of piracy to provide an engaging and insightful analysis of a whole new breed of online intermediaries that's transforming how fans discover new bands and participate in their success."
Nancy Baym, www.onlinefandom.com and Associate Professor of Communication Studies, University of Kansas

Net, Blogs and Rock 'n' Roll

How Digital Discovery Works and What It Means for Consumers, Creators and Culture

David Jennings

NICHOLAS BREALEY
PUBLISHING

LONDON · BOSTON

For my parents, Roy and Julia Jennings

First published in Great Britain by
Nicholas Brealey Publishing in 2007

3–5 Spafield Street
Clerkenwell, London
EC1R 4QB, UK
Tel: +44 (0)20 7239 0360
Fax: +44 (0)20 7239 0370

20 Park Plaza, Suite 1115A
Boston
MA 02116, USA
Tel: (888) BREALEY
Fax: (617) 523 3708

www.nicholasbrealey.com
www.netblogsrocknroll.com

© David Jennings 2007
The right of David Jennings to be identified as the author of this work has been asserted in
accordance with the Copyright, Designs and Patents Act 1988.

ISBN-13: 978-1-85788-398-5
ISBN-10: 1-85788-398-5

British Library Cataloguing in Publication Data
A catalogue record for this book is available from the
British Library.

Library of Congress Cataloging-in-Publication Data
Jennings, David, 1965-
    Net, blogs, and rock 'n' roll : how digital discovery works and what it
means for consumers, creators and culture / David Jennings.
        p. cm.
    Includes bibliographical references and index.
    1. Music and the Internet. 2. Music trade. 3. Internet marketing.
    I. Title.
    ML3790.J45 2007
    780.285'4678--dc22

2007024107

Printed in Finland by WS Bookwell.

Contents

Discovery...

When recorded entertainment was hard to get hold of, fans used to dream of having vast libraries of audio and video material at their fingertips. Thirty years ago, the range of records you could buy outside major cities and specialist shops was limited, and when it came to visual entertainment you got what the broadcast and cinema programmers wanted to give you. A few fans were committed enough to put in the time and effort to find out about material outside the mainstream and then to track it down, but neither of these tasks was easy and these dedicated detectives were the exception.

In the twenty-first century we live with an economics of abundance in music, television, film, and games. The internet has made it possible to track down almost anything, legally or illegally, with a few clicks of a mouse. We have what fans used to dream of. There are many more routes—from blogs to reference sites to online entertainment stores—that lead us to new material and let us try it out on demand. We are seeing a profound change in the way we make cultural discoveries. In the digital age everything is available, with each item vying with the millions of others, old and new, that can be found in the unlimited expanse of the internet. Our problem now is scarcity of attention.

If you want to explore new music nowadays, you might check out iTunes, subscription services like Rhapsody, free advertising-supported services such as Napster or Qtrax, and tens of thousands of niche online radio stations, unlicensed file-sharing sites, or artist videos on MySpace and YouTube. Then there are the services popping up everywhere on the net that analyze what books, music, and films you like and generate a personalized list of recommendations. Some even put a kind of robot DJ in your computer or digital music player that sequences a playlist for you, adapted to your tastes and moods. When friends recommend a band or a film, you can find out more by consulting a reference site like allmusic, or perhaps pay a visit to Wikipedia, an online encyclopedia where anyone can chip in and contribute their expertise.

All of these routes are part of the digital discovery process. With the expansion of on-demand access, coupled with the richness of information and perspectives that comes with blog culture, we are crossing a watershed. We do not have to depend so much on coincidences to discover new entertainment that will tickle our individual fancies. We do not have to go out on a limb by making risky purchases, or wait for recommendations from friends. The digital means of research are within easy reach to even the most casual of consumers: reviews and audience ratings, historical and career context, lists of related material, and samples of the material itself.

The central focus of this book is on music discovery—how it has changed and how best to respond to these changes—because music is a bellwether for other forms of entertainment in many ways. The fan economy for music has been around for a long time. It is richly developed within different genres and age groups. The challenges of unlicensed file sharing hit music first, and its fans have embraced blogging and social networks in a big way. The intelligent filtering technologies for making automated personalized recommendations of stuff you might like to check out are most advanced in the world of music, because they have more data to build on. Most of the problems—and the solutions—in terms of digital discovery are coming to music first. And where music leads other media may follow: audio and video downloads on iAmplify; television on Tape It Off The Internet; venues and events on Eventful and Upcoming; ebooks on Fictionwise; travel advice and experiences on RealTravel.[1]

The challenges of the fan economy

...**Many aspects of** the era of abundance are highly desirable. It offers the enticing prospect of a "celestial jukebox" where you can pull down almost anything you can think of from a digital store in the sky and listen to or watch it at your leisure. But, as with many significant changes, it also brings disruption and challenges. Google may promise to index and organize all the world's information, creating a reference source of almost God-like omniscience, but having information organized for you is one thing; deciding what to look at next is another. This is what could be called the "problem" of discovery, and it manifests itself in different ways for different groups: the creators of entertainment, its consumers, and the services that connect them.

As creators, whether we've just made a multimillion-dollar film or a three-song demo recording, we want to know how to attract and hold the attention of an audience that is bombarded with choice and, once we have hooked them, how we can get our fans to spread the word and build buzz. As consumers we have to struggle to keep up with everything that's going on and balance friends' recommendations with media hype and our own idiosyncratic hunches. Finally, as professional reviewers, broadcasters, and those in the new breed of digital stores and services, the problem is how to shift gears from being the gatekeepers that we were when consumers had only to decide between Tower Records and an independent store, *Rolling Stone* and the *New Musical Express*, *Top of the Pops* and *MTV Unplugged*, to being facilitators of the interaction between entertainment and consumers in an era of infinite choice. As media enterprises we need to understand all these changes so that we can develop strategies to meet them head on.

Unsurprisingly, there is no single solution to such challenges. We pick up the scent of discovery in many different settings, online and offline: from reviews, discussions, and stories, from personal recommendations and recommender systems, from overheard exchanges, and from the unusual radio station that was playing one time in our uncle's kitchen. Because we pick up leads in anarchic ways and all over the place, there can be no *one* service that provides an all-encompassing discovery solution for music, film, books, games, or other domains.

Perhaps the most significant shift that comes with the economics of abundance is that now we are spoilt for choice in ways to discover new entertainment, the tables have turned in terms of who makes the running. Consumers are no longer sheep who can easily be herded toward some Next Big Thing that has been hatched up in the studios and marketing departments of television companies, radio stations, and Hollywood. The means by which we can find out about interesting new material are limitless. Mainstream television and radio, press, even Amazon and Yahoo! have to live in a world where we can switch our attention elsewhere in a few clicks. The producers will seek to shepherd us toward their offerings, but when it comes down to it, all of us are free-range explorers.

Net, blogs and rock 'n' roll

...The potent combination of advances in technology and the laissez-faire culture of sharing discoveries is what creates the *Net, Blogs and Rock 'n' Roll* recipe. The net provides a platform where data, content, and comment can be combined and made available to multiple audiences by multiple routes. Blogs provide the diversity and participation in spreading buzz, fueled by individual, authentic voices and relationships between people. Rock 'n' roll injects the attitude and the appetite: the sense that life is too short to spend time waiting for every *i* to be dotted and every *t* crossed. The energy comes from the hips as well as the head—discovery and exploration are never ending.

The *Net, Blogs and Rock 'n' Roll* recipe helps us make sense of the potentially disorientating and ever-evolving landscape of discovery. Instead of looking out through a restricted window, like the porthole on a large ship, we can all be on the bridge, with a 360-degree view and the captain's prerogative to steer in whatever direction we choose. More than that, the copy-and-paste capabilities of digital media and Web 2.0 enable us to remix what we see and re-present our own versions of it. Songs are no longer welded to the fixed sequence of a vinyl groove, but can be mixed with others from different sources in a playlist, or used to soundtrack home movies.

The technologies known as Web 2.0 provide a platform that enables and accelerates social explorations, which reach into corners of our culture that mass media have largely ignored. Many of us like *some* popular hits, but we also like quite a lot of "non-hits" (it's just that we all like *different* non-hits, which is why they are non-hits). In his landmark book *The Long Tail*,[2] Chris Anderson charts a dramatic change under which sales are no longer so exclusively concentrated on current hit titles but are distributed across a wider spectrum, right down to the tail end of the charts where, thanks to infinite digital shelf space, even obscure titles are better able to find niche markets. This brings with it a whole new set of business challenges.

No one is in charge of digital discovery. Blogs and the "tearable web" are wrenching the reins from professional media (whose ties with producer industries are sometimes perceived to be too cosy), making it easy to share opinions, and easy for fans to help each other. The defining characteristics of blog culture include:

...An open form of mass participation in media where anyone can contribute.

...A conversation, not a lecture or a broadcast—there is no "final word."

...No commissioners, no editors, self-publishing with no infrastructure of control.

...Mostly a noncommercial activity (corporate blogs and mainstream media blogs exist, but are arguably not what the ethos of blogging is really about).

...The fan economy is a gift economy, rewarded by recognition and in-kind returns from fellow contributors.

...A focus on the individual, authentic voice.

...Part of a wider activity of personal networking, finding like-minded souls, and building communities of interest.

Fans and the entertainment industries that service them have to adapt in order to tap the riches of this era, and understanding how discovery works is fundamental to this. Consumers can learn how to exploit and integrate the unprecedented sources of discovery at their disposal. Creators can help their work find its market and tap the energies of fans in spreading the word, generating new revenue opportunities in the Long Tail. Media businesses can learn the multimethod techniques that lead to discovery in order to build their profile with fans and grow their revenues. Online and broadcast companies and the press can come to an understanding of how the landscape has changed, how discovery has moved to center stage, and how they can best inform and engage with free-range consumers when their role as gatekeepers for discovery is on the wane.

Against this background, DIY and independent creators are well placed to benefit, partly because they have less to lose by licensing their material, and also because the costs of setting yourself up and finding a potential audience are falling all the time. Garageband.com is one such grassroots DIY endeavor, aimed at helping musicians and fans help each other. Members can upload their own recordings, provided they agree for these to be heard by other members and licensed for inclusion in podcasts without charge. Members' reviews and ratings provide feedback to the artists, as well as creating charts of the popularity of different artists and tracks. From there it's a case of "survival of the fittest," as the songs with the best ratings get most exposure to Garageband.com users and stand a better chance of being discovered. What is being created through Garageband.com (and similar sites like Jamendo and Amie Street³) is an amateur economy that in some ways parallels the mainstream music industry, with its own bands, critics, DJs (podcasters), fans, and charts.

How to read this book

...Throughout the book I use the metaphor of foraging for interesting material, which, with the associated idea of picking up an "information scent," depicts the way discovery can involve either an extended search or a happy accident when you catch the smell of something good blowing on the breeze. It also captures the fact that discoveries frequently depend on mixing together information and clues from many sources. The first chapter gives examples of what discovery looks like in practice and how it works on the net.

Part II outlines how in the fan economy people are taking discovery into their own hands. While some fear that iPod culture is cutting people off from each other by enclosing them in their own personalized cocoons, we will see how communities of consumers come together and how the volunteer effort of even small numbers of committed fans can inform and influence others. Tracking what other people like is a key way of picking up the scent of new discoveries, and everything from blogs to charts can help with this.

In Part III we look at the changing role of intermediaries between creators and their audiences, from critics to the new breed of social networks and recommender systems that aim to help us make discoveries. We'll explore how analysis of the "genetic" make-up of music can help match discoveries to your personal tastes, and how blog culture and "crowdsourcing" can augment traditional broadcast and written media, rather then replacing them.

Part IV shows what new technologies and techniques are speeding the journey of discovery: how Web 2.0 adds a social dimension to searching and browsing, while buzz marketing methods encourage bloggers and fans to spread word-of-mouth recommendations. This part brings together the previous chapters into the *Net, Blogs and Rock 'n' Roll* recipe for discovery.

The final chapters review the implications for consumers, creators, and the media—and for our shared culture.

Please read the book as though foraging for your own cues and clues on how digital discovery works. The themes and patterns that jump out at you will depend on your interests, and you can dig deeper via the resources signposted in the Notes and the blog at www.netblogsrocknroll.com.

Part I
The scent of discovery

1

Use a little TLC...

Imagine a table with all the cheeses of the world arranged on it. How should you approach such a potential feast? Some cautious people will spend a great deal of time hunting through all the varieties to find the ones they know and like. At the other end of the spectrum, there may be pioneers who try to sample as many different cheeses as they can in a short amount of time. Soon, however, they find that their palate is unable to absorb or appreciate any new tastes, and they have to give it a rest. There will be those who join with friends and sample a few cheeses before exchanging views and recommendations on what each has found. A few will lurk and overhear what others are saying, noticing patterns as someone finds a cheese they particularly recommend and more people cluster round, some staying or passing on the recommendation while others demur and drift off elsewhere. Another handful of people may wait to see which are the overall Top 5 most popular cheeses before making their own selections.

Foraging for information

...Discovering music, films, games, or books is not quite like cheese, but all the above patterns of behavior—and more—do occur to some extent. Variety in methods is the norm. We can compare it to foraging for food in the animal world.

Foxes, squirrels, and seagulls display different kinds of foraging behavior: individual, carnivorous scavenging; hoarding food to enjoy later; and large-scale flocking. Bees do a "waggle dance" that helps other bees find the way to sources of pollen. Wild goats leave tracks to feeding patches that other goats can follow. Although seagulls don't compile charts of fish and foxes don't write reviews of chicken coops, foraging activities do find human parallels, for instance in blogs that, like a waggle dance, point the way to something new and interesting, or in playlists and listening behavior leaving a trail that links one known source of music to another, unknown one. We have evolved a rich set of signs, charts, and commentaries to guide each other through the cultural world.

If you're looking for entertainment and there are only a handful of possible places to get it (a few radio or television stations, a magazine, and your local store, let's say), then you take what you can get from these sources. But if there are thousands of sources and your time and attention are limited, it's a different story. In that case you either fall back on instinct and habit, or you get to grips with which sources to explore further, how to evaluate them, and how to get the most out of the promising ones.

This is foraging—making your own way, doing it yourself. Being a fox, a squirrel, or a seagull, rather than an easily herded sheep. Of course, foraging behavior is not completely new as a means of discovering unfamiliar music, films, books, or other entertainment. Truly dedicated fans have always been prepared to devote time to hunting down rarities, but for the rest of us this degree of commitment was more than we could justify for pursuits that were little more than a passing interest.

The internet and blog culture have brought some of the excitement and rewards of self-directed discovery within the reach of anyone. It is easier now to trace the links between artists you like and others you may not have heard of. It is easier to find information about artists you don't know about, and easier to try out their work. It is easier to locate and participate in groups of people who share an interest in these artists.

One of the useful things about the information foraging metaphor is that it puts an emphasis on individual, self-motivated exploration, but also allows for the many social influences and cues that make their presence felt in the process of discovery. The social cues include blogs that give directions: "Here, this way, there's something good at the end of this link" or "This stuff smells like sheep food to me; not my kind of thing." They're also in filters and recommendation systems that say: "People who bought what you're looking at now were also interested in this stuff over here" or "If you like that track, may we recommend some others that would complement it nicely in a playlist?"

Another helpful feature of the foraging metaphor is that it captures a mix of intentional and incidental discovery. Many people have an almost instinctive response to the question of how to find things out: start with Google. But while Google and other search engines do indeed provide rich resources for exploration, sometimes we don't know what to search for, or we haven't even considered that a search might be possible or useful.

Incidental discovery often turns into intentional discovery, and vice versa. You start off by incidentally stumbling across a reference to a band, a writer, or a film maker that somehow catches your interest, and that becomes the starting point for a new journey, where you intentionally set out on the trail of more information, and you ask your friends what they know. Or you may visit the Amazon website or the iTunes Store with the intention of getting something specific, and a tempting suggestion catches your eye and inspires an extra detour on the way to your destination.

Jennings' law

...**The idea of** an information scent, as a means of helping users follow a path to find what interests them, has influenced web designers in recent years, after it was first described in information foraging theory. This theory has been developed over the past decade by psychologists and computer scientists at Palo Alto Research Center.[4] It also gave rise to the concept of "information patches" to describe the way we switch our attention from one patch or source (a website, group forum, online store, radio, or television station) to another. The internet and search engines make it so quick and easy for foragers to switch between patches that if they lose the scent of something interesting for even a moment, they will be off somewhere else in an instant. Usability expert Jakob Nielsen advises web designers not to fight this tendency toward short periods of "grazing" interspersed with switches of attention, but to design sites and services that support the activity as effectively as possible.[5] Make it easy for people to take quick snacks, he says, find ways to encourage them to return, and, above all, maximize and optimize the ways in which people can find you.

In many ways this is the opposite of the traditional marketing injunction to make your website "sticky," in an attempt to capture your users' attention for as long as possible. But the two goals need not always directly conflict with each other. As Amazon and the iTunes Store show, you can support quick transactions while also providing users with enticing diversions that may hold them longer than they planned, despite their scarcity of attention.

Discovery isn't something you turn on and off, any more than you can stop and start looking while your eyes are open. Sometimes you do it in a more focused, concentrated way than at other times—and some people are more focused more of the time, thanks to their particular enthusiasms and obsessions. But, because discovering things is a natural function of our brain and something we remain open to all our waking hours, it's hard to see how any one source—let's say Google, Amazon, Microsoft, MySpace, or Wikipedia—could monopolize even a substantial proportion of our discovery time. Jakob Nielsen has coined his own "law" of internet user experience: "Users spend most of their time on *other* sites than your own."[6] This is an important consideration for website designers, and for anyone designing a resource to help people make discoveries.

My own take on this is Jennings' law: "People make most of their discoveries elsewhere." The designer's aim is to enable free-range foragers to follow up the discoveries they make elsewhere using your resources as effectively, easily, and enjoyably as possible, and to inspire further related discoveries.

TLC: Trying out, Links, Community

...When we set out on any journey of discovery, we depend on all the cues and clues we can get to help us find our way quickly to the most interesting areas. Wayfinding signs, maps and photographs, a compass, advice from fellow travelers, and evidence of paths well trodden—all of these could prove useful.

The spread of always-on broadband access to the internet has brought with it three primary elements that are ideally suited to supporting discovery:

> ...Trying out, or auditioning, material by hearing a sample, viewing a trailer, or downloading a limited version.
> ...Links.
> ...Community.

Discovery can start with any of these ingredients, though it frequently involves more than one of them. If you want to help people make discoveries, create your website or blog with TLC, enabling users to braid together these three strands to support their foraging.

Trying out

The economics of abundance are nowhere more apparent than in the scope there is to sample entertainment. Instead of what used to be limited opportunities to try out television and music programs, we now have YouTube, MySpace, and music subscription services (Napster, Rhapsody, and Yahoo! Music Unlimited, for example) that provide catalogs of more than a million tracks on demand, in return for either a monthly subscription or some exposure to advertising. More controversially, defenders of unlicensed peer-to-peer services for sharing audio, video, and interactive files argue that many of the downloads from these services do not substitute for sales, but are used for try-before-you-buy auditioning. Add to those the burgeoning number of services on related platforms—mobile, wireless, satellite, digital television, and radio—that offer further opportunities to try out entertainment before you commit.

MySpace (www.myspace.com) fueled its early growth by making deals with content owners. This helped promote both the content and MySpace's social networking platform, rapidly attracting large numbers of teens and young adults. If you were a member of MySpace in Autumn 2004 you could hear the new R.E.M. album, streamed over the net, before anyone else did. Similar exclusives with a new single from Oasis and a Black Eyed Peas album followed, and, with the rapid rise in membership that these engendered, MySpace became *the* platform on which both new and established music acts felt they needed to have a presence—thus creating a snowball effect that attracted yet more members.

However, you don't get to try out music on MySpace without first arriving at someone's MySpace page, and you don't get there unless someone or something has tipped you off that it might be worth checking out. What if you don't have any tip-offs and you still want to discover and try out new music? That's where personalized online radio-style services like Last.fm (www.last.fm) come in. Last.fm asks you to name a band or artist you like and will then play you a stream of music by similar artists. As you listen to this stream—your own interactive radio station—you can indicate for each track whether you love it or can't stand it (if it's just OK, you don't have to do anything, except listen). This helps Last.fm build up a profile of you as a listener and gradually refine what it plays you. The basic service is free and is licensed through record labels, distributors, and collecting societies (who distribute the royalties they collect to rights owners).

Last.fm, which was acquired by CBS for $280 million in 2007, is driven by a music "engine" that tracks the music all its members play, and manages the large collection of music profiles that result from this tracking. The music you hear is based on the preferences of other Last.fm listeners who share at least some of your tastes, known as your "neighbors." So, if you say you like 50 Cent, Last.fm may play you a track by fellow rapper 2Pac, based simply on the fact that the engine has noticed how many other listeners who like 50 Cent also like 2Pac. The two artists may actually have little in common musically, but that doesn't matter as long as their fan bases overlap. This kind of recommendation service—known as collaborative filtering—may be familiar to you through services like Amazon's "Customers who bought books by Writer A also bought books by these writers..." listings.

Links

Links have always been used to aid discovery—as, for example, when someone reviews a film using comparisons: "It's like *When Harry Met Sally* crossed with *Speed*." But the World Wide Web is *made* of links, and so it takes discovery by browsing to another level. I've said there is no such thing as a one-stop solution for discovery, but the closest thing to such a solution is probably the web itself. Its beauty is that if you're searching for information in one place and not getting much of what you want, or if you catch the scent that tells you another place might be more useful, you can be there in a matter of seconds.

Reference sites like collaborative encyclopedia Wikipedia and allmusic (www.allmusic.com) are prime sources that enable you to delve deeper and wider into the areas that interest you. Allmusic prides itself on being "the most comprehensive recorded music reference available," covering all classical and popular genres. At the time of writing, one of the "Editors' Choice" selections is the *West* album by the singer-songwriter Lucinda Williams. Clicking on Williams' name brings up a web page full of many kinds of links. There are links to other artists with whom she has worked. But allmusic is more ambitious in nudging people who like Lucinda Williams to find out more about other artists whom the site's editors consider to be related to her in some way. The site provides a kind of family tree of influence, showing the ancestors (the people who influenced Williams), the descendants (her so-called "followers"), and her siblings (what allmusic calls "similar artists"). Williams has recorded many cover versions of other artists' songs, so the list of links to artists whose songs she has performed gives further pointers to the gene pool of her music. If that wasn't enough, allmusic has also classified the mood of her music in terms of more than 20 adjectives from "warm" and "yearning" to "organic" and "earthy." Again, these adjectives are links that take you to, for example, the top 10 "earthy" albums and songs.

Allmusic has sister sites called allmovie and allgame covering these entertainment media. Allmovie groups films into genres like "romantic drama," "action thriller," and "musical." They are also assigned tones like "stylized" and "sentimental," and even moods like "high on emotion." There are links to similar movies and (where applicable) to movies with the same cast or production staff.

These reference sites were built for surfing. They are designed for free-range foragers who wander through information space driven by their interests. This self-motivation is a big factor in the discovery and exploration of new entertainment in the digital age, as we will see throughout this book. The allmusic site will not do much for you if you don't bring your own curiosity to the game. You may pick up some new information from your initial search, but it is through active exploration of the links on each page that you start to unravel relationships between different bands and identify patterns—for example when you keep finding the same band that you've never heard of listed under "similar artists" for several of your favorite albums.

Community

Community, the third strand of TLC, is the motor of the fan economy. The multifaceted relationships between fans drive the ways in which they share opinions and recommendations. Again, the internet has brought about a step change in how people find communities of like-minded fans, how they interact with them, and how their opinions are distributed and aggregated. In recent years social networking technologies have also shown how communities can organize information for the common good, through sharing tags and playlists, as we will see in a moment.

It's via word-of-mouth recommendations that a buzz develops about particular artists, songs, films, books, or games. Word of mouth turns out to be a very potent way of breaking into the big time, especially if the buzz reaches a tipping point where it starts to spread under its own momentum—when the sheer volume of recommendations becomes unavoidable, even to those with just a passing interest, and itself generates further positive comments.

While reference resources like allmusic have to assume that their users will be curious, active, and self-motivated, the community aspect of social networks like MySpace (along with its competitors like Bebo, Facebook, and imeem) provides an incentive for mass participation. Not only do fans love to pass the word around when they find games or music they like, but they are also motivated by the kudos that comes from being the first among their peers to discover a new or little-known band. On the receiving end, we tend to be influenced by the recommendations of friends and trusted acquaintances as much as—or more than—by the recommendations of professional but impersonal sources such as press reviews or reference sites.

Last.fm adds a community dimension to its service by letting you listen to the personal radio stations of friends and strangers as well as your own. You can join special-interest forums and, as with many social networks, post your thoughts and opinions in a blog on your public profile.

Last.fm also encourages its users to "tag" an artist, album, or track with a classification that they think might be useful to them in the future. These tags can be reasonably objective, like "1978" for the year a track was released; widely accepted terms, like "disco" for the genre of the music; more impressionistic, like "energetic" or "precious"; or entirely private, like "commute" for music you want to listen to on the way to work, or "Paul's birthday party" for a track you want to include in a playlist for a friend.

Tags serve two purposes. At a purely personal and selfish level, you can use them to organize your listening. You can "tune" Last.fm to play just the artists you have tagged as "disco" when you're in that mood. But at a community level, anyone can read and use the tags that others have assigned as well as their own. So if you haven't tagged anything as "disco" yet, you can start with the radio station of tracks that *other people* have tagged with this term. This social tagging is known as a "folksonomy," a term denoting a taxonomy or classification that is derived from folk wisdom, with all its attendant shortcomings of herd mentality combined with lack of oversight and maintenance (this is still contentious in some circles, as we will see in Chapter 5).

Playlists are another way of organizing and personalizing digital entertainment. By compiling your own playlist of songs or videos, you can make a sequence that both suits your own purposes and expresses your "take" on the music and videos concerned. Sharing your playlist with others is a way of publishing your opinions and expressing your identity, while also giving the rest of the community a trail they can follow to make their own discoveries.

Playlist sharing has its roots in the hobby of recording tracks from a personal record collection onto cassette "mix tapes" to give to friends. This has long been recognized as an enjoyably social way of passing on music recommendations. But whereas circulating mix tapes infringes copyright ("home taping is killing music" went the slogan a quarter of century ago), online playlists can be shared without such infringement and still provide a means for others to discover, and purchase, new music.

For example, MyStrands (www.mystrands.com) is another digital entertainment social network that works by tracking what its members listen to. As you play tracks, you can add particular selections to a playlist and then publish the playlist for other users to listen to, comment on, and tag—just as though it were an album in its own right. Or you can create a playlist using iTunes software on your computer and upload it to MyStrands. Whereas compiling a mix tape was a labor-intensive activity restricted to serious fans, the "drag-and-drop" ease of digital tools brings playlists within the reach of even casual listeners.

Playlists also have a sustained fascination for readers, listeners, and creators. As the critic Paul Morley wrote in *Words and Music*:

> The list is what brings a world of chaos into some
> kind of pattern... Everyone loves a list for making
> sense of the awesome nature of all the stuff that
> surrounds us.[7]

In the context of the increasingly convenient online access to millions, or tens of millions, of music tracks, that awesome nature and volume of stuff is becoming all too apparent. This may be what led David Goldberg, when he was General Manager of Music at Yahoo!, to claim, "the playlist is the killer [application] in music."[8]

Playlists are one example of how people trade tips and recommendations in the fan economy. Amazon also encourages its customers to create lists for other media including games, DVDs, and books, and MySpace members can post their own audio and video content and share it with other members. Millions of short clips add to the richness of the site (after all, MySpace itself originates a negligible proportion of the material it hosts) and stimulate discussion and personal contacts. The clips include educational and instructional material as well as music videos and trailers for movies and games.

Braiding the TLC strands

This book is not going to fall into the kind of technological determinism that assumes that just because there are some clever things you can do on computers, in a few short years everyone is going to be using those things, and only them, to find out about music and movies (there is a good chance that at least one of the websites mentioned above will be on a downslide by the time you read this, such is the turnover in internet services). The point is that these resources *add to* rather than substitute for the ways you discover entertainment. It's not an either/or scenario. We mix and match between established and digital methods like magpies, taking the best from both.

Online or offline, we braid the strands of TLC—we try stuff out, we follow links, and we trade recommendations among a community of fans. We chat to friends about music and television programs in bars, perhaps with a live band or a jukebox playing in the background; we consult reviews in the general and specialist press, as well as documentaries on the radio, on television, or on DVD. We trace the links created by celebrity endorsements and tie-ins with movies, games, and advertisements; and, last but not least, we absorb the traditional marketing activities of music and film industries by trying out their material via television and radio airplay.

The specifically digital elements of discovery come into play, first, because the universe of music and entertainment has expanded and we need all the help we can get to sift through everything. And secondly, because the TLC strands provided by the likes of MySpace, allmusic, and Last.fm help us make discoveries more quickly, more effectively, and in a way that is better tailored to our individual interests.

As we follow any of the TLC strands, we cross back and forth between online and offline worlds. Traditional reviews, broadcasts, and promotions can integrate digital TLC strands to give them more reach and power. For example, a book about the New York alternative rock scene in the 1980s may be accompanied by an online playlist of all the tracks it cites as influential; it will be referenced by the profiles of relevant bands on allmusic and Wikipedia; it may be discussed on the alt.rock message boards and email lists; and it will have a website aggregating its reviews in mainstream publications and blogs, as well as providing links to resources for further foraging.

The development of what is known as Web 2.0 will accelerate this integration between digital resources and traditional media channels. The Web 2.0 techniques and standards make it easier to clip different bits of software and data together like Lego bricks, so that, for example, a single web page can pull together trailers and reviews for movies showing locally, samples from bands playing this weekend, and photographs from a current festival, even when each of these elements originates on other sites. Bloggers are already taking advantage of Web 2.0's mix-and-match approach to incorporate their own and others' images and sounds on personal websites without needing any sophisticated technical skills. I will be looking at this in more depth later in the book.

Free-range foragers

...**In the new** era of discovery, fans are free-range foragers. The designers and architects of services to support their foraging must take account of the full range of TLC methods by which they find out about music, films, games, and books. Maps and reference sources like allmusic and allmovie may be part of the solution. So, too, are community-focused sites such as MySpace that provide the means for fans to flock together around the things that interest them. There should be scope too to follow the "tracks" and links that others have left behind them, as in Last.fm and MyStrands.

In addition to this, designers and web architects have to bear in mind that whatever they do and however sophisticated and elegant it is, there will always be a desire on the part of some fans to "grow their own." These are the people who produce blogs and wikis that enrich their own experiences and also create valuable resources from which others can learn and discover.

It is to this variety in consumer behavior, and how it fuels the fan economy, that we turn in the next part of the book.

Part II
The fan economy

2

The vibe-raters...

As **consumers, listeners,** and viewers, we are not all the same. Some of us are massive film fans, some are music nuts, and others are only casually interested in either. Our differences are reflected in the level of energy and the preferred approach we have to discovering new entertainment. These differences drive the fan economy, from how people trade recommendations (if a friend of yours is a film fanatic, you can call her up to see which of the new releases she rates highly) to how they organize more or less spontaneously to take part in joint activities, from a cultural evening out to building a fan website.

This chapter focuses on diversity among music listeners, who frequently demonstrate almost tribal differences of allegiance between fans of various genres. It's music that young people have used most to express their identity, and it's in this area that the most detailed research has been done. We will look at the variations in how people collect entertainment, how likely they are to invest time in actively curating and sharing their collections, and how committed they are to discovering new material.

Collecting and curating

> Yeah, it took me quite a while to put this whole project together because some of the tracks are from my own records but most of them are from

other Depeche fans and I've also this website where I've put all the scanned CD covers and some background information on who recorded the remix, and where it was released.

This is a quote from Martin, a committed Depeche Mode fan, as reported in research carried out by Markus Giesler, assistant professor of marketing at York University in Toronto. Giesler interviewed several users of the original Napster (unlicensed peer-to-peer file-sharing) service.[9] Martin has scouted out a large number of tracks from several sources, and Giesler observes how he talks about the process of preparing and providing his special Depeche Mode music collection to other Napster users. It almost seems that for Martin, the music files themselves are not as important as the combination in which they are presented. Martin wants this playlist sequence to symbolize his expert identity among other fans, and Giesler describes how such a playlist can "function to establish and maintain social relationships with other users."

In today's on-demand world where there is access to vast volumes of music, video, and other entertainment, everyone becomes their own curator. They make selections from large libraries and then sequence, arrange, or prioritize them. This personal management of large volumes of digital "assets" is still an emerging area, and Giesler's work is one of the fairly rare attempts to understand what is going on when people collect and curate their own entertainment. (The fact that many of the most prolific collectors and curators have, like Martin, procured or shared their collections illegally does not make it any easier to bring these behavior patterns out into the open.)

Research in the UK—which has a strong music culture, with the world's highest number of albums bought per capita—estimates that the average number of CDs in a personal collection is between 126 and 178.[10] Music buyers are getting older or, put another way, the habit of buying music is extending to older age groups. In 1999 music buyers over the age of 30 still accounted for a minority of music sales in the UK, but by 2005, 55% of sales were made to this older group.[11] In the same year in the US, 25% of music was bought by over 45s.[12] 2002 was the first time that people in the 40–49 age range bought more music than those in the 12–19 range.[13]

It's hard to find equivalent figures for DVDs and games. Because the formats and markets are not so long-established, it has been harder to build substantial collections. Films on videocassette and games for older-generation consoles become harder to play on new hardware and may be discarded. But beyond these historical and technical factors, the nature of our relationship with films, television programs, and games is different from our relationship with music. We buy music for repeat listening and may play favorite songs of the moment several times a day, while we still treasure classic older albums decades after we bought them. Few people play DVDs repeatedly within a short period, and although games are addictive in the short term, their shelf life is often more limited than that of music.

In his erudite book *The Recording Angel*[14] on recorded music and the people who cherish it, Evan Eisenberg puts forward five reasons for us collecting cultural objects:

> ...The need to make beauty and pleasure permanent—to be able to hear your favorite music or see your favorite drama whenever you want it.
> ...The need to comprehend beauty—to be able to study the performing arts through repetition.
> ...The need to distinguish oneself as a consumer—to express individuality through taste.
> ...The need to belong—including using music and video as part of nostalgia for past experiences.
> ...The need to impress others, or oneself—either through outright cultural snobbery or some more subtle variation.

Not everyone feels the need to impress fellow fans, and they don't mind if their collections have gaps. Behind the statistics for the average size of a music or DVD collection there is a wide variation: a few are many times greater than the average, and many are much smaller. Some of the more fanatical file sharers seem like squirrels who compile large hoards of music or video— often more than they can listen to or watch in a reasonable period—almost as though they expect winter to arrive at any moment and deprive them of the opportunity to collect any more. Others are more like butterflies who flit from one passing enthusiasm to the next without ever worrying about keeping things for tomorrow. Are you one of the fanatics who strive always to be ahead of the game, or do you wait to see which way the herd is going and then follow?

Project Phoenix

...**In 2003 and** 2005, media company Emap set out to research and map the fan economy, including the different groups within it, their attitudes and behavior. Emap owns 3 UK music magazine titles,[15] 27 radio stations (analog and digital), 7 digital music television channels, and 17 music websites. Its research, commissioned under the title Project Phoenix, was designed to help its advertisers target promotions on its media channels.[16] In 2003, the researchers surveyed the views of 2,200 15–39 year olds who completed a detailed questionnaire about their music-listening and purchasing habits, as well as other related lifestyle and attitude traits. These were supplemented by 30 in-depth focus groups on the subject of fans' relationship with music. Late in 2005, a second survey was carried out to identify changes and trends in the data.

Emap's Project Phoenix divided people into four tiers of interest in music, from the indifferent to the fanatical, and then abstracted some more detailed portraits of subgroups within these tiers. Excerpts from these portraits are in Table 1.

SAVANTS Everything in life seems to be tied up with music 7% of the 16–45 age group (down from 9% of the 15–39 age group in 2003)	*Example identifying characteristics:* • Being knowledgeable about music is central to "who I am" • You reckon you could write better questions for the local bar's music quiz *Example subgroups:* • "Insiders"—males in their mid to late 20s who are often in bands themselves • "Curators"—males in their early to mid 30s who are self-declared aficionados of good music • "Hoodies"—mainly teenage schoolboys living at home with their parents
ENTHUSIASTS Music is a key part of life but is balanced by other interests 21% of the 16–45 age group (up from 16% of the 15–39 age group in 2003)	*Example identifying characteristics:* • Believe that the iPod has made the world a better place • Get more of a kick from hearing a favorite song on CD than watching its video on television • Less "purist" in their musical tastes than savants *Example subgroups:* • "Miss Dynamites"—knowledgeable, worldly wise and "sophisticated" mid to late teen girls • "iPod tourists"—mostly males in their 20s with a passion for niche music, using it to define moods and occasions • "Party Grandees"—males in their late 20s to mid 30s who still put an active social life ahead of adult responsibilities
CASUALS Music plays a welcome role, but other things are far more important 32% of the 16–45 age group (up from 26% of the 15–39 age group in 2003)	*Example identifying characteristics:* • Got into Coldplay about the same time that Gwyneth Paltrow did • Equally, or more, interested in the lifestyle and fashion trappings of the music world than the music itself *Example subgroups:* • "The Glamour Club"—music plays an important functional role in their lives but it's not something they give much thought to

	• "Weekend Rowdies"—males and females in their mid teens to early 20s who live for the weekend • "Mums in touch"—women in their 30s with busy lives who want to "keep up" and not be boxed in by their age or parenthood
INDIFFERENTS Would not lose much sleep if music ceased to exist 40% of the 16–45 age group (down from 48% of the 15–39 age group in 2003)	*Example identifying characteristics:* • Most of the songs they hear at parties sound unfamiliar • Tend to listen to talk radio or sports rather than music (No subgroups identified)

Table 1 *Excerpts from Emap Advertising Project Phoenix results*

You won't be surprised to see that the subgroups within the Savants tier are defined mostly in male terms. In fact, in the younger segment of the age group (15–24 years), males outnumbered females by only 54% to 46% in 2003. But as people grow older, there is a tendency for women to drop out of the Savant tier so that it becomes much more male dominated in the older segment (82% of 25–39-year-old Savants are male). To a lesser degree there are similar trends in the Enthusiast tier, with women's interest in music declining with age.

While numbers of Savants and Enthusiasts seem to drop off with age, the increasing buying power of those who stay the course seems to compensate—which may be one reason increasing proportions of music are bought by older people. Overall, Savants and Enthusiasts account for only a quarter of people in the 15–39 age group, but this minority undoubtedly accounts for a majority of music listening and sales. Inevitably, these tiers will also be the main focus of attention here.

One or two further points are worth noting about the classifications in the research. They represent a snapshot in a particular country—the UK—at a particular time. Such categories are always evolving, and the classification of subgroups shown in Table 1 may not apply in different countries (even if it seems likely that the distinctions between the four main tiers of interest would hold good more or less universally). Whether or not the subgroups are empirically watertight does not matter for the purposes of this chapter (though it may matter for advertisers), because the main point here is simply the *existence* of different groups. The finer points of the groups' nature may be up for debate, and my use of such points in this chapter is therefore partly speculative.

The central point is simply to illustrate how people with varying kinds of interest in music discover and explore it in different ways. Music listeners are not an undifferentiated mass. Neither are film fans, game players, or book lovers. Once we see beyond this, we can map the roles that different kinds of fans have in discovering entertainment and passing on word-of-mouth recommendations.

Alternative approaches to music discovery

...From the Project Phoenix data it's possible to abstract the various ways in which people discover music, according to the nature of their interest and the role that music plays in their life. For example, the research asked about factors that influenced the music people bought. Unsurprisingly, the Savants and Enthusiasts were much more likely to be influenced by reviews in music magazines, or by hearing music for the first time at festivals or gigs, compared with the Casual and Indifferent tiers. This section paints some speculative pictures of how different groups of listeners go about their discovery, including the extent and areas of their foraging.

Insiders

Let's take the Insiders group within the Savants tier first. Music is their life. They see themselves as the "true" fans of music for music's sake and set themselves apart from anything that smacks of hype or commercialism, which they view as polluting the pure musical instinct. By contrast, live music represents the most authentic expression of that instinct, and the Insiders are devoted to it. They immerse themselves in music and every part of their life—the company they keep, the books they read, the television they watch, and the places they go—works toward this end. Many Insiders are in bands themselves and celebrate the communitarian lifestyle of the gigging musician, in the hope that one day they will be able to give up their day job (which may well involve working on the fringes of the music industry).

Music discovery for Insiders may be purposeful or incidental. It's purposeful in the sense that Insiders would have thought nothing of reading the 550 pages of Simon Reynolds' *Rip It Up And Start Again: Post-Punk 1978–1984* immediately after it was published, partly so that they would not be left out when it came up in discussion at the next gig. They might enrol in a course in rock history if one existed—if only to correct the lecturers' mistakes. And they are always on the trail of new left-field releases and overlooked classics from the Long Tail of specialist niche titles.

Living the way they do, the Insiders cannot help discovering music by accident as well. They could be at their own band rehearsal when the bass player brings in a copy of an obscure Weather Report track to illustrate the sort of feel he thinks the rhythm section should aim for when playing the band's new composition. Or they could be at one of the summer festivals and stumble across an act that none of their friends has heard of, playing on one of the smaller stages, leading to them becoming instant fans of that band (and taking every opportunity to proselytize about them to their friends).

Because of the emphasis they put on hearing music for themselves and making up their own mind, Insiders would say that trying out (the T in TLC) is their favored way to discover new music, rather than following the mainstream buzz of marketing hype. They are prepared to put in the time to listen, sometimes quite intently, to new music. Their listening is highly focused and targeted at sources they can trust. They seek out particular radio programs and DJs rather than just having the same station on all day in the background; they swap compilations or playlists with fellow fans, rather than browsing aimlessly by genre. One way in which a site like MySpace appeals to the Insiders group is that it provides them with the scope to play the scouting part of the music industry A&R (artists and repertoire) role on an amateur basis. Insiders enjoy the idea of grassroots discovery of unsigned acts, before the industry gets hold of them. They also like the kind of personalized discovery service that Last.fm offers, and will put in the effort required to "train" the service by frequently inputting their preferences and thus building a finely tuned profile.

However, because music is the focus of Insiders' social life, their trying out is mediated by their community of friends. This mediation has both cooperative and slightly competitive elements. Music is central to an Insider's identity and one way they can distinguish themselves in their circle of friends is to be the first to discover a hot new act. So Insiders always have an ear out, even if only subconsciously, for something they can pass on and "break" to their mates. However, any element of one-upmanship is more than balanced by the emphasis on music as a collective pastime. Playing music, listening to it at gigs, and sharing knowledge and recommendations about it are all fundamentally social activities for Insiders. These activities blur seamlessly between face-to-face and online (internet and mobile) spaces. Insiders are usually members of many global email groups and web forums dedicated to particular artists or genres of music, and these are used as a platform for organizing local meet-ups for like-minded fans, particularly at relevant gigs.

Links to related music are also part of the currency of the Insider community. As well as being frequent visitors to music websites—including allmusic, but also more specialist sites like eMusic (www.emusic.com) and Boomkat (www.boomkat.com)— Insiders may publish their own blogs about music, or work as part of a group maintaining a fan website. Through these activities, Insiders again show that they are not willing simply to be on the receiving end of an "authorized version" of the music scene and music history. They are keen to present their own version of the scene, their own playlists, and—as we will see in more detail in the next chapter—to *create* associative links as well as to follow them.

Curators

The Emap research suggests that Insiders are "confident and strident in their criticisms of the current music press and feel it has very little to tell them." By comparison, fellow Savant group the Curators are more likely to be devotees of the media, from the specialist press to music television documentaries. Notwithstanding the rise of the net, sales of specialist "heritage-focused" music magazines are on the up, and it seems to be mainly the over-30 music fans who are buying them.

Of the Curators, the research says, "They tend to rely on old trusted musical choices rather than engage with anything new or emerging—as a result, they now look backwards to fill the gaps in their collection rather than forwards to discover new music." They sound like curmudgeonly-before-their-time men in middle youth, whose music "is generally very tangible—all vinyl and CDs that can be touched and admired rather than a collection of de-materialised files on a hard disk."

This could be one area where the Emap data is showing its age. In 2003, when the first stage of the research was done, there was no iTunes Store in the UK, and opportunities for legal downloading were few and far between. In 2005, the British Phonographic Industry reported that 96% of money spent on music downloads came from men, and nearly 40% of these were aged between 35 and 44,[17] suggesting that there are plenty of early adopters of digital music in the older age range. Clearly, the usage patterns in this area are in a state of rapid flux, with the legal download market growing from 20 million tracks globally in 2003 to 200 million in 2004, and 795 million in 2006.[18]

If the Curators do indeed read the heritage magazines— such as Emap's own publications *Q* and *Mojo*—then these provide an avenue for music discovery that may fit both their interests and their lifestyle. As I write, the *Q* cover feature is on the 30th anniversary of punk rock (the celebration of which seems a paradox that any punk would have disowned 30 years ago), *Mojo* has the Kinks on the cover, and there's a new 148-page special edition of *Mojo Classic* devoted entirely to rare and unseen material about the Rolling Stones. Since anyone in even their late 30s now would not have reached puberty when punk was at its height—let alone when the Kinks and the Stones were in their prime—these publications genuinely represent heritage for readers from an age group that did not experience the music when it was first released. Their interest is fired not by nostalgia for their youth, but by an interest in the grand sweep of tradition and the "classic" artists who defined the shape of current popular music.

Combing the vaults of the past is one of the tasks these magazines set themselves, but it is not the only one, and their readers are presumably interested in more than merely a history lesson. As well as helping in the reappraisal and revival of "lost" recordings and artists, magazines like *Mojo* provide lots of reviews of reissued recordings and new releases. The genres they cover may not stray further from mainstream rock than, say, reggae and Motown—perhaps to suit the conservative tastes of their Curator readership—but more adventurous connoisseurs of music can find other specialist magazines such as *The Wire* and *Songlines* that cover niche genres.

As aids to exploring music, these publications are the periodical equivalent of reference sources like allmusic. They provide the in-depth contextual and critical information to guide and complement the music you try out through other sources. Increasingly, they are branching out to provide ways for you to try out music as well, via cover-mounted CDs and radio on the net. In the not too distant future, we can expect to see more partnerships between these publications and specialist, editor-led online stores like eMusic, leading to a multiplatform approach.

Curators thrive on this combination of music and the detailed information that puts it in context. They are also the prime target market for boxed sets, the in-depth retrospectives of an artist's career or a themed collection, spread over several CDs with a booklet of original text and pictures.

The Emap research suggests that Curators no longer go clubbing and may even go to gigs less often than they used to— possibly due to parental responsibilities—so their relationship to music is increasingly a domestic one and, if not solitary, certainly less social than the Insiders' living-and-breathing-music experience.

However, in the age of the internet, being more tied to the home does not stop people engaging in the broader cultural conversation. The research found that the older Savants were more likely than other groups to report using the net to find information on their hobbies and groups. Generally, they were also more motivated by creating things and setting trends, or being influential, among their friends. The Curators may channel these energies into playing a lead role in an online fan forum, perhaps building a database of their favorite band's set lists for a website, or running their own music blog. The next chapter explores those creative impulses in more detail.

Hoodies and Rude Boys

The Hoodies and Urban Rude Boys in the Emap research are on the borderline between being Savants and Enthusiasts. Mostly teenagers in both cases, they have perhaps not quite had time to hear enough music to graduate into full-blown Savants. Keen to catch up and "get an education," these groups' appetite for new music outstrips their wallets. Having grown up with the net, they are prime candidates to resort to unlicensed file sharing to explore what's worth collecting. The research quotes one Hoody: "15 quid for a CD or 25 quid for broadband and all the music you want..."[19] (However, encouragingly for the recording industry, the 2005 follow-up research found many instances where young fans did switch from unlicensed to legal digital music as they got older and had more money and less time.)

Being part of the net generation, these groups are reported to spend a lot of time reading blog reviews and recommendations, but the Rude Boys are also very visual and are reported to use music television, along with the internet, as a primary source for music information and discovery.

Enthusiast groups

As with the Savants, Enthusiasts' preferred methods of finding out about music vary with age and gender. One group is dubbed the Party Grandees—men in their late 20s to mid 30s who have not yet retired to domesticity—and for them clubbing and gigs are the favored ways of checking out new dance music, backed up by browsing the net and downloading.

The iPod Tourists are a group with eclectic tastes, reflecting the use they make of music to create a soundtrack to many different parts of their lives—not just nightlife—and are increasingly keen to explore the great music of the past. According to the Emap research, they have lost patience with the established music press on the grounds of its "insincere hype" in building up and knocking down new scenes. Increasingly they, and other enthusiasts in their mid 20s, adopt a promiscuous approach to music media, which has the net at its centre but may also include specialist music radio and television.

The Miss Dynamite group shows another approach again. These teenage girls apparently see the mainstream pop market as not niche or trendy enough for them, and use music to differentiate themselves from their peer group and stake out a more adult identity. Community and word of mouth are central to their music discovery. They effectively create a small sub-culture with their friends and exchange music recommendations through debate with each other and the older music fans with whom they identify.

This role of music in forging youth identity and community is well documented in social science research.[20] A recent study by psychologists documents how teenagers enthusiastic about music "preferred to display their individuality by claiming tastes that they did not associate with 'the masses.'"[21] The psychologists analyzed interviews with music fans between 13 and 16 years old and they outline individual case studies:

> [John] listened to Nirvana initially in order to claim a "rebellious" and "cool" identity, but later stopped when "everyone else" started to listen to it as well—he wanted to avoid the imputation of just being "one of a crowd" of fans... His change of taste towards what he calls "weird stuff" (he later explains that it is a genre called industrial music that he is referring to here) communicates to others he is distinctive and unusual. By explaining how "challenging" and "weird" it is, he also claims an identity as a knowledgeable music listener—he can appreciate the type of music that "those who just want to kind of sit there" with music on purely as a background wouldn't understand.

The dynamics of community are complex here. Certain very popular music gets branded by the teenagers as being for the "sheep in the flock" and is therefore to be avoided. Knowledgeable music listeners create an in-group. They pass recommendations between themselves but, as we saw with the Insiders, they gain kudos among their friends by being the first to discover new music—especially the "weird stuff." In order to do this, they have to do some solitary research and discovery, using the net, radio, and other channels. Meanwhile, there is the ever-present danger that yesterday's weird stuff may not be weird enough and may become tomorrow's chart fodder, undermining its value as a tool to distinguish oneself from the masses.

Casual and Indifferent groups

It goes without saying that such self-consciously elitist attitudes are anathema to casual music listeners. They probably would not recognize themselves as "sheep" either. Nevertheless, casual listeners are often content to rely on the market and the charts to filter what new music they hear.

The young adults that the Emap research calls the Glamour Club have a strongly consumerist approach to music. They won't spend a lot of time reading about music either in print or on the internet. To the extent that they use the net for music, it is very much for on-demand transactions (rather than discovery): searching for and downloading a track via an online store or file-sharing service. Trying things out via radio and television is their main source for new music. Fashion conscious in a different sense from the Rude Boys mentioned above, their approach is also dominated by images rather than words. According to the research, "their main priority is to keep in touch with the newest chart hits, know more about their favourite artists and stay abreast of the latest gossip."

In general, while music is the center of attention for Savants and Enthusiasts, it occupies the background for Casual listeners, part of a broad sweep of entertainment culture that includes celebrity gossip, reality television, and style tips. While Savants and Enthusiasts may choose their friends based on what music they like, Casual listeners are more likely to choose their music based on what their friends like. Music provides some of the juice that lubricates their social life rather than being the axis around which their social life revolves.

For the Indifferent tier of music listeners (around half of the population) the same applies as for the Casuals, only more so. Music may be the bridesmaid to another activity but never the bride.

The various attitudes to mainstream chart music shown by the most committed quarter of the population (Savants and Enthusiasts) compared with the other three-quarters (Casuals and Indifferents) creates another complex dynamic in the way new music percolates through the audience. In the crudest terms, the minority of committed fans act as scouts, both in the vanguard and on the fringes of mainstream taste. They discover new acts, some of whom may pass into the mainstream sooner or later (as well as Nirvana, R.E.M. and Radiohead arrived by this route) while others remain on the fringes, known only to the cognoscenti. Those that do pass into the mainstream risk losing some of their credibility with the self-appointed opinion leaders, in return for a much broader audience.

Meanwhile, other acts aim to bypass the music "snobs" and target the mainstream audience directly, using channels that appeal to them, such as reality television shows. While new acts have taken the *Pop Idol/American Idol* route to an audience, the celebrity version of *Big Brother* in the UK has seen existing bands like the Ordinary Boys and the Towers of London attract wider mainstream attention via the nonmusical exploits of their members.

In summary, the way the music audience breaks down shows a wide range of habits and behaviors that influence the music we listen to and discover. While we all inhabit the same landscape, the ways we go about foraging for what interests us are as different as the approaches of squirrels, magpies, butterflies, and, indeed, sheep.

In the next chapter, we will look at the impact of those whose creative impulses encourage them to stake out the landscape, to provide discovery resources for others, and thus potentially to emerge as opinion formers and leaders. Then, in Chapter 4, we will look at the role of charts and other measures of consumer behavior in digital discovery, including how they give clues to new trends, point the way to the Next Big Thing, and thus make it easier for others to follow.

3

Fans as creators...

Andy Aldridge is what you might call a card-carrying Savant. He's never actually been in a band, though he's been learning to play the piano for the past four years, and his day job is in the BBC Archives. Always a fan but never an extrovert, for many years in his youth Andy lacked a network of other fans with whom to discuss his enthusiasms. Now he is at the center of a group of nearly 400 such fans, having invested his technical and creative skills in building his own web archive dedicated to his favorite band, Galaxie 500, and all the other bands and duos in which its members have gone on to perform.

Andy's site (www.grange85.co.uk/galaxie) carries an extraordinary amount of detail—for example, a discography with details of each song, cross-referenced to set lists for each live gig where the song was played—much more than you could ever find on any official site, on allmusic, or via any other source. The website was created in 1994, and a year later Andy added an email group to enable all the fans who had contacted him to communicate with each other. It is through the dialog in this email group that I, among many others, have been kept up to date with the activities of the Galaxie 500 musicians, have been prompted to find out more via the website, and have discovered the music of similar bands via recommendations from fellow fans. This range of resources and community dialog represents a not unusual example of how an influential part of the fan economy works, and how it catalyzes new discoveries.

We will come back to the community aspects of how a group of fans start to cluster together later in this chapter, but for now I want to concentrate on the creative and leadership role played by the most committed fans.

People like Andy collate, coordinate, and filter the information they come across. Then they organize and interpret it to make it easier for others to digest. They are doing more than just pointing the way to good foraging ground. They are farming and refining, making a patch of ground more fertile.

The unpaid work that Andy does in bringing together such a rich range of information and pointers could be win–win–win for a number of people. First, fellow fans, especially "beginners," can gain a mine of useful indicators to which albums they might want to explore, as well as an overview of an extended network of musicians from the same stable. Second, the bands concerned clearly stand to benefit from having someone who plays the roles of both archivist and informal fan club moderator (they have given Andy permission to reproduce some of their copyright material; some of the band members participate in online discussions; and they invited Andy to manage the official Galaxie 500 MySpace page on their behalf). Andy's site is *the* online destination that does most to maintain and support fan interest, and to encourage catalog sales. Finally, any third-party platform that hosted or licensed Andy's material would enhance its offering to its users. So far, the closest example of this is the MySpace Galaxie 500 page (www.myspace.com/galaxie500official), which includes an automated "feed" of news from his own site, as well as edited highlights from that site and the usual audio and video clips.

A pyramid of influence

...It's understandable that a lot of people in the marketing and media industries are interested in identifying, encouraging, and—if possible—enlisting influential members of the fan community like Andy Aldridge. In *The Tipping Point*, Malcolm Gladwell introduces the idea that certain key people can act as what he called "Connectors, Mavens, and Salesmen" in spreading ideas and starting word-of-mouth epidemics.[22] Paralleling this terminology, the buzz marketing sector has coined various bowdlerized terms such as Alphas, Influentials[SM], and E-fluentials[23] to denote the minority of influential thought leaders.

In the context of driving business growth through corporate brands, Sven Rusticus refers to Brand Advocates, the people so satisfied with their experience of a brand that they will promote it to others under their own steam.[24] He distinguishes them from Brand Adorers, who are loyal but not so vocal, and Brand Adopters, who are just regular users. He represents these three groups as a pyramid, reproduced as part of Figure 1, to show that the Advocates are smaller in number but significant in their influence and impact. This is where the parallels with degrees of activism and leadership in online communities get interesting, and a link can also be made with the Savant/Enthusiast/Casual/Indifferent classification in the previous chapter.

On his blog, Bradley Horowitz, vice-president of Product Strategy at Yahoo!, reports that just 1% of users of the Yahoo! Groups online community services actually animate their groups by starting them or initiating new discussion threads.[25] This compares with 10% who make modest contributions, frequently in response to someone else, and, of course, 100% who are assumed to read material contributed by others (though nine out of ten of them "lurk" without participating). While Horowitz refers to these three groups as Creators, Synthesizers, and Consumers respectively, I use the terms Originator, Synthesizer, and Lurker (to avoid confusion with the different senses in which creator and consumer are used in this book). He also represents them as a pyramid—included in Figure 1—

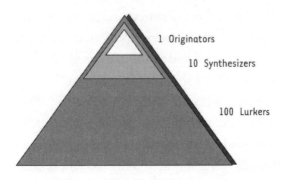

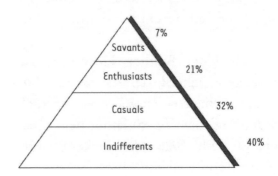

Figure 1: *Pyramids of influence and activity*

Top pyramid adapted from Rusticus, S. (2006) "Creating Brand Advocates" in Kirby, J. & Marsden, P. (2006) *Connected Marketing: The Viral, Buzz and Word of Mouth Revolution*, London: Butterworth-Heinemann. Middle pyramid adapted from Horowitz, S. (2006) "Creators, Synthesizers, and Consumers," http://www.elatable.com/blog/?p=5, 17 February.

though in this case the different categories are nested within each other, as each creator is also a synthesizer and a consumer of other people's contributions.

Is it in fact possible to overlay the categories from the Project Phoenix data on these pyramids, as I have suggested in Figure 1? It's clearly not the case that every Savant is an Originator. Not all Savants are confident or concerned enough to create original material related to their favorite music. But they don't have to be. The scale and reach of the net are such that we need only a minority within a minority group to be active in order to create rich and sophisticated material—like Andy Aldridge's site—that other fans can productively explore. If only one in seven of the Savants is interested in contributing something original to the fan community, and even if their contribution is just an interesting new topic of discussion rather than a comprehensive site, then the figures still tally sufficiently to generate a sustainable stream of useful material.

The values of Savants also coincide considerably with the characteristics of blog culture, as defined earlier in this book. We saw in the previous chapter that the Insider group of Savants places strong emphasis on authenticity, individual "grassroots" voices, sharing of opinions and content, and building communities of interest. Thus a proportion of them are "natural" bloggers.

So there seems to be at least some consistency between the three pyramids in Figure 1. It may be a moot point, however, whether a pyramid is always the right way to represent these different levels of commitment, activity, and interest. Horowitz refers to his pyramid as representing value creation. Those few at the top do more to create, maintain, and animate online communities than do the relatively passive larger group at the bottom. His point is that communities do not require majority participation in order to be successful and to generate content and relationships that their members find valuable. Indeed, the pyramid could instead be an iceberg, with 10% visible and the rest lurking out of view.

Nevertheless, while someone at the top of the pyramid may be more influential than an individual at the bottom, there are many more people at the bottom, and it would be dangerous to infer that influence flows in only one direction. People define themselves and their tastes as much by what they're not as by what they are. As we saw in the previous chapter, some Savants explicitly react against what they perceive to be popular among the Casuals and Indifferents who represent mainstream opinion. Such opinion is rarely expressed in confident word-of-mouth recommendations, but tacitly, via the shopping basket. (Hence, for example, the phenomenon of artists and bands that achieve significant sales while it is rare to find anyone who will publicly admit to liking them.)

Another point to emphasize is that these figures and fractions apply *within* particular communities but not right across the population. No one is saying that only 1 percent of people on the net create original or influential material. Many of us are Originators in the fields that most interest us, Synthesizers in others, and just Lurkers in the areas we are casually interested in. The way we distribute our creative energies is similar to the way attention and sales are distributed across the entertainment market, and one man's Big Hit is another man's Long Tail obscurity.

Originators and synthesizers join forces

...So what are the ways in which Savants or Enthusiasts can express themselves and demonstrate some leadership across the fan economy? Blogs are one obvious route, and they can be used both to originate and to synthesize. Many blog posts point to other websites and, indeed, to other posts on other blogs. In doing this, they digest and synthesize the web, making it more comprehensible to other like-minded people. Gradually, clusters of bloggers emerge, reinforcing each other and developing a loose network of affiliated people and ideas.

In line with Bradley Horowitz's original focus on Yahoo! Groups, another way you can participate creatively is through email or web-based groups. You might either instigate a new discussion—let's say, write a review of a new film you've just seen that connects with the group's interests—or react to the opinions of others. A lot of discussion in online groups is also a kind of collective synthesizing and digestion of relevant news: new releases, tours, series, or appearances.

On blogs and online discussion groups, different opinions sit side by side. You can remain independent of others and agree to disagree. In wikis like Wikipedia, it's a different story. A wiki is a website that allows its users to add, remove, or otherwise edit all (or almost all) the content on its pages. The wiki approach seeks to merge different voices to arrive at a coherent consensus statement. This means that over time, the pages become collaborative endeavors, drawing on the knowledge of several contributors.

In keeping with blog culture, wikis reverse the traditional publishing model of "expert writes, everyone else pays." In Wikipedia the theory is that anyone writes and no one pays.[26] In practice, though, as with other areas of online creation, it turns out that only a tiny minority of people do write. Wikipedia's own figures suggest that the number of active editors and contributors is between 0.5 and 4% of registered users, depending on the measure of activity—and a significant proportion of Wikipedia readers are not registered.[27]

In 2004, I created the original Wikipedia entry for a particular album, 69 Love Songs by The Magnetic Fields. In the following two years it was edited over 50 times, though the main descriptive text in the entry remained substantially the same as the first version. About ten of these edits were minor corrections and updates that I made, but the others were contributed by a range of other Wikipedians and mainly related to standardizing the entry to make it look more like those for other albums: adding a track listing, adding categories and a chronology to position the album among others, adding links to other entries, and correcting the format of citations to conform to the Wikipedia standard.

It seems this is a common pattern on Wikipedia. People contribute blocks of information in areas where they have significant expertise (Originators), but then a large number of small edits are made that put this information in the right context and presentation format (Synthesizers).[28] In this case, then, it's actually the Synthesizers who are the most regular editors and the Wikipedia "insiders"—much like a traditional magazine or reference source, where a core staff would edit and lay out the work of a much wider but looser group of contributors.

If you're in any doubt about the importance and influence of the material generated by fans on blogs and wikis, consider the cases where mainstream entertainment adapts in the light of what fans say about it online. The cult ABC TV series *Lost* provides one example. It's impossible to quantify reliably the mass of commentary and reaction that this series has generated, but it's a lot. This includes the Lostpedia site (lostpedia.com), which is explicitly modeled on Wikipedia but concerned exclusively with the series, as well as an ABC official wiki (lostwiki.abc.com). Lostpedia provides episode-by-episode synopses, profiles of the characters, details of locations, and analyses of recurring themes. Though most of the links on the site refer within the *Lost* universe, some also point outside, as in the catalog of appearances of literary works in the series.

In his blog article "Why *Lost* is genuinely new media,"[29] Dan Hill refers to these kinds of sites as metamedia, existing as they do in a critical symbiosis with the original media content for which they provide commentary. The idea of such commentaries is itself not new. Companion works to guide audiences through the finer points of Shakespeare's plays have been published for centuries, for example. But there is a spectrum from editor-led, one-way reference works through to editor-free, community-led dynamic sites (this spectrum is the central topic of Chapter 5).

Hill indexes a massive array of online discussions about *Lost*—of which Lostpedia is just the tip of the iceberg—and argues that the collaborative nature of these enterprises amounts to a kind of "social life" of the television series, such that it "uses the entire web as its canvas and its entire audience as its creators." The audience (or, as with Wikipedia, a small but committed percentage of the audience) picks up the elements of the programs and uses them as a currency for conversation, speculating about possible plot explanations. And these conversations may, Hill suggests, feed back into the development of the series.

The games industry takes this even further, and several commentators have asked whether multiplayer games like Second Life point the way to a future where the consumers—if that is still the right word—are actively involved in creating the experience they enjoy.[30] Second Life enables its users to create their own artefacts and even their own businesses within the virtual world of the game. Players retain intellectual property rights in their virtual creations, and some make a tidy profit from their endeavors. There is a risk of overgeneralizing from a medium that overtly expects you to be an active participant to other media—film and recorded music, literature, or broadcast—that give you more limited scope for interaction. However, the fundamental point remains. Communities of fans naturally self-organize into Originator, Synthesizer, and Lurker roles, and there is a cycle of influence between these roles that can significantly affect the word-of-mouth reputation of a book, film, piece of music, or game.

Communities of practice

...**As we look** into the details of how groups coordinate their shared activities within the fan economy, we start to see how supposed leisure pursuits take on many of the characteristics of the world of work, particularly in terms of the division of labor. The difference, of course, is that no one is giving orders in these groups, and there are no contracts in place to ensure continuity and loyalty to common goals. But the fans have what every employer aims to instill: a shared commitment that comes from *inside themselves*. And via the net—with its communications channels of blogs, wikis, and messaging—they can develop large-scale resources together.

In their shared and active commitment to music or video, fans can sometimes demonstrate similar achievements and similar ways of learning from each other to those that you might find in a workplace. The development of Lostpedia is an example of such an achievement. Research into how learning spreads between people engaged in shared activities refers to the groups concerned as "communities of practice." These share some activity-oriented purpose, which plays a part in defining their identity within the group. Typically communities of practice include both core and peripheral members—the core members being the "old hands" while the peripheral members are serving a kind of informal apprenticeship.[31]

Andy Aldridge may have been the instigator of the Galaxie 500 website and email list, but he's at pains to point out that there's a lot more going on among the fan community than the activities he initiates, and that the community that has grown up around these channels is by no means "his." The fans have—among many other things—contributed set lists and photographs from concerts around the world; worked out the guitar chords for most of the repertoire of songs; recorded and privately distributed their own tribute album; and researched the feasibility and costs of producing a privately distributed vinyl release of a CD-only album. For a while, another community member operated a server where live recordings were collated and shared. (Some of these activities have involved sharing of copyright material; the community was in touch with the bands' members and withdrew any material to which the performers objected.[32])

By doing things together over time—the "practice"— communities of practice achieve several things. First, and most obviously, they get things done: creating a free public listing of performances by a band, for example.

Secondly, they develop a shared way of working together, what leading theorist Etienne Wenger calls a "shared repertoire of resources: experiences, stories, tools, ways of addressing recurring problems."[33] In the case of the Galaxie 500 community, this would include when (and how) to use the server, experiences of previous "flame wars" on the email list and how they were resolved, the ethical codes of what is and is not legitimate digital copying, together with shared memories of meet-ups at gigs and which albums have topped the fans' polls over the years. Andy Aldridge observes that none of the people who were active and vocal in the community ten years ago (with the exception of himself) is still active today. But the character of the exchanges has stayed remarkably similar despite the changes in personnel. This is the power of collectively and tacitly understood customs.

Thirdly, learning and discovery are inevitable by- products of these shared practices. The activities may be led by the core members of the community, but over time the other members get the hang of things, either simply by lurking on the email list or by playing some supporting role that justifies the core members showing them the ropes. Andy surprised me when I met him by telling me that word-of-mouth recommendation via the email list he started is one of the main ways in which he discovers new bands. So influence does not just flow from the head of the pyramid to its base.

Finally, and perhaps most importantly for a community of music fans, the extended period of doing things together gives a sense of collective identity linked to their favorite bands. This is helped by the fact that, in the case of the Galaxie 500 email discussion list, various members of the bands have themselves been part of the list, sometimes passing on the latest news about albums and tours from the horse's mouth, and even offering their own guest-list passes to community members who traveled long distances for a farewell gig.

In common with many active fan groups, the Galaxie 500 online community has evolved into a self-organized and self-regulating channel for communications, support, and learning, which reflects again three levels of commitment, similar to Originators, Synthesizers, and Lurkers. The Originators look after the technical and social infrastructure of the community. In return for this unpaid work as ambassadors for the band's music, they may enjoy personal relationships with the band and other "gift economy" favors such as being invited to after-show parties. The Synthesizers back up the Originators' efforts with moral support and occasional offers of practical help. Through this process they develop the competences to take their place in the core group of Originators if necessary. Any Lurker members will initially just be passive members on the periphery of the online community. Over time they may grow in confidence or be drawn into group discussion and activities, thus graduating to become Synthesizers; alternatively, they may pick up a little useful information and then just leave.

A sustainable community of fans manages the ebb and flow of core activities in such a way that it maintains a stream of information and exploration to keep the majority of its members interested. In the gaps between album releases and tours there is only so much trivia and fan polls that can keep discussion flowing. In these circumstances, the Galaxie 500 mailing list follows the practice of many other online forums in discussing music by other bands that fans might like. Any member of the list might suggest a new band to discuss, and before long a canon of other bands that are frequently mentioned emerges. Thus the community becomes another channel whereby new music can percolate between Savants and Enthusiasts and on to more Casual listeners. As well as the community aspect (the C in TLC), this process also demonstrates discovery through associative links, since every band discussed on the Galaxie 500 email list is implicitly linked to Galaxie 500.

The canon of bands linked to Galaxie 500 by the fan community overlaps with the lists of similar artists in the Galaxie 500 allmusic and Last.fm entries—all include Low, Yo La Tengo, and The Feelies, for example—but the former also includes other bands that are personal favorites of core members of the community.

Playlists and personality

   ...It takes only a small minority of active users, then, to create valuable resources and sustain a thriving community. The likes of Yahoo! and Wikipedia can take consolation from this. But that doesn't mean that they wouldn't like to encourage a greater proportion of their users to become active. Happily, technology is taking some of the creative activities that used to be the preserve of professionals and Savants and making them easier for more casual fans to get to grips with, while social networking sites are providing the motivation to create as a means of personal expression.

   Tagging is one example, because the new services mean that it is a cinch to tag images, songs, and web resources. A recent study found that 28% of US internet users have tagged content online,[34] reinforcing the point that such practices are not limited to small numbers of Originators and Synthesizers who go round organizing everything on the net. Another example already touched on earlier in the book is the creation and sharing of playlists. One way of looking at these lists is as trails that foragers leave behind them to indicate to others a rewarding and fruitful path through the mass of available material.

Cultural insiders and curators have been creating lists of books and art for centuries. From the 1970s music Savants and Enthusiast fans used the new cassette format to produce mix tapes of their favorite songs, which they passed around (sometimes with hand-drawn cover art and extensive sleeve notes) in order to turn their friends on to their latest discoveries. Sometimes I used to edit multiple fragments of a few seconds between songs to create an aural collage; making a 90-minute mix tape of this kind with analog technology could be a day's work. Using the drag-and-drop technology of Apple's iTunes software, I can compile a 90-minute digital playlist in about a minute. I can then upload that list to one of many playlist-sharing websites to get feedback and ratings from friends and fellow fans. Thus playlists come within the reach of Casual, or even Indifferent, music listeners.

In his book *iPod Therefore I Am*,[35] Dylan Jones shows some of the potential of the playlist format when he imagines what would have happened if The Beatles had not split after the release of the *Abbey Road* album but had gone on to record one further album in 1970, titled *Everest*. He provides a track listing for the album, which he has compiled for his iPod using songs written by each of the four Beatles around 1970 and subsequently released under their own names. Jones also writes the story of how the album came about, how George Harrison persuaded the others to postpone the split of the band, how John Lennon argued for the inclusion of one particular track, and how George Martin, as producer, held the ship together. Jones concludes, "*Everest* is just one example of how an entire oeuvre can be reconfigured using iTunes, how a whole career can be re-examined, re-edited and born again."

As well as giving us an insight into music tracks themselves, playlists often seem to open up another window on the person that created them. That's why celebrity playlists are popular, with Apple introducing them to the iTunes Store in its early days, record labels commissioning celebrities to make compilation albums, and radio stations hiring everyone from Bob Dylan to Courtney Pine and Lulu as DJs for specialist shows. Not waiting—or not wanting—to be hired, David Byrne streams his playlist from his website (www.davidbyrne.com/radio).

Many Savants really go to town on their playlists, displaying the fruits of extensive research. Ernest Paik is a Chattanooga-based fan of the songwriter Stephin Merritt, an artist who is himself distinguished by his scholarly knowledge of musical traditions and his willingness to reference multiple cultural sources in his work. For a year, Ernest published his Stephinsources MP3 blog (stephinsources.blogspot.com) in weekly instalments. Styled as "the songs that inspired the songs about songs," each instalment introduced one or two new artists, provided details of how Stephin Merritt had cited or drawn on their work, and provided the means briefly to try out a couple of their songs. Over time the blog grew to become a scholarly reference source, intricately hyperlinked to the interviews, profiles, and other documentation on which it drew, and an extended essay on a particular aspect of Merritt's creative practice. It was also a fictional celebrity playlist.[36]

Software like iTunes makes it possible for listeners much less committed than Ernest Paik to compile playlists, almost without thinking about it. The desire to project your own identity, and to sneak insights into other people's tastes, is what drives a lot of playlist sharing. This was shown graphically in the case of 13 co-workers, all based in the same office, who were able to browse each other's music collections using their company's internal computer network.[37] Researchers at the Georgia Institute of Technology and Palo Alto Research Center found that these people, some of whom did not know each other well, consciously worked to portray themselves in certain ways through the collections of music they chose to share. In one example, a participant was anxious about what his colleagues would think of him in the light of the Justin Timberlake and Michael McDonald music that they could find on his computer. He had purchased it, he said, "for his wife."

The researchers demonstrate how people use music to manage the way other people see them, an area of identity management that was defined by Erving Goffman's sociological classic *The Presentation of Self in Everyday Life*.[38] Because music is an imprecise way of communicating your personality, and because this group of co-workers also included a mix of Enthusiasts and Casuals with different musical interests and knowledge, the self-portrayals were sometimes misread by colleagues. Nevertheless, as the research showed, the activity of music sharing helped to build a community within the workplace as the co-workers came to find out more about each other.

Several software applications and web services now exist that make it easy to compile lists of books, films and videos, or games, and then publish them online for friends and strangers to peruse. These each have the same narrative and essayistic potential as music playlists, in the way that they encourage people to make associative links between different items, and it is equally possible to try to "read" an acquaintance's or a celebrity's personality from such lists. What is not so feasible—with the exception of short films or videos—is to cue up a playlist of books and games, press "play," and enjoy the results in a reasonably short period.

What the examples in this chapter begin to illustrate are some of the ways in which cultural discoveries are transmitted through groups of people. Some groups come together explicitly for the purpose of discussing music or entertainment and keeping up with what's going on. These groups can develop a strong and persistent sense of community—and generate practical, useful information in the process—with just a minority of active participants.

Most of us also belong to other groups (at work or elsewhere) that have nothing to do with culture or entertainment. But the ease of sharing playlists and other collections of favorites via the net can encourage mutual exploration of each other's tastes. In this case we're driven not by curiosity about music or films *per se*, but by the opportunity to find out more about our neighbors or colleagues. And in the process of doing that, we find out more about music, films, books, and other stuff.

4

Wise and foolish crowds

Small **numbers of** Originator fans wield a disproportionate influence on others through the leadership they display and the opinions they express in blogs and forums of all kinds, but the silent majority can also affect each other's behavior. They do this indirectly through the charts that are compiled from that behavior. Humans are deeply social animals, and we can't help but be influenced in the directions our paths of discovery take by what other people think. Charts provide us with clues to tell us what others consider valuable or interesting. This chapter shows that we have an increasingly broad range of charts at our disposal, and how these influence us, both as consumers and creators.

Charting new territory in an on-demand world

...In the heyday of the Top 40, the pop charts were one of only a few ways we had to measure what other people liked. What's more, they combined elements of narrative and interactivity. The narrative developed as a song entered the charts and started a week-by-week climb that might progress in leaps and bounds, or in tiny steps. At some point the song would peak, hover for a week or two, and then begin its decline, to be replaced by the next set of releases—a classic cycle of heroism and decay. The interactivity came from the mass participation in buying 45 rpm records, which felt like voting for your favorites. When the Boomtown Rats' single "Rat Trap" was No. 2 in the charts, I bought a copy purely in an attempt to help it to No. 1, given that I already had the song on their album. (My purchase probably wasn't made in one of the stores that provided sales data for the charts, but happily "Rat Trap" made it to No. 1 anyway.)

If there's an equivalent mass-participation format with the same narrative and interactive elements today, it's probably the television talent show, where you register your vote with a phone call, a text message, or a click, rather than the purchase of a record. The traditional sales-based Top 40 is in crisis, having to manage long-term decline in sales of singles and increasingly complex rules about what a single *is*, and having to compete against television and radio airplay charts, club charts, and many other varieties. It has lost its "water-cooler effect" status as a topic of public discussion. First it lost its narrative drama as the release strategies of new singles meant that almost all songs reached their highest chart position in the first week of release, and then went down from there. At the start of 2007, the UK Official Charts moved to address this by including all downloaded songs regardless of release date, with the result that a six-month-old song immediately re-entered the Top 10. If John Lennon had not been killed in 1980 and had died, instead, when his solo and Beatles catalogue was available in download stores, it's not inconceivable that every song in the Top 20 would have been one of his compositions.

Meanwhile, some of the new digital charts turn out to be even less inspiring. The top five artists of the month on the MyStrands service at the time of writing are, in descending order, The Beatles, Coldplay, U2, Red Hot Chili Peppers, and Green Day.[39] Who are the hot new rising stars among these? Well, since the top five was exactly the same last month, no one can really lay claim to that accolade. The story is similar on other services.

The top five artists on Last.fm this week are, again in descending order, Red Hot Chili Peppers, The Beatles, Radiohead, Coldplay, and The Killers—also with minimal change week on week.[40]

These top-level charts are not where the action is. They're not exciting enough to draw in casual fans, and they're of very little use as an aid to discovery and exploration.

The MyStrands and Last.fm charts are not based on sales; they're based on actual numbers of listens. That's one reason they're so static. There is some music that people keep coming back to, while other music is more ephemeral in its appeal. You lose the tacky novelty hits, but you lose the drama as well. If and when future generations have their equivalents of hits like *Dark Side of the Moon*, *Thriller*, or Crazy Frog's "Axel F," their *Empire Strikes Back* or *Last Emperor*, it may be that charts will show not just week-by-week sales but also give some indication of the "active life" of each sale. This would measure how often, and for how long, people keep listening to music or watching films after their first exposure to them.

Digital services also collect other data to capture what people think of the music they listen to and the films and television they watch. In different ways, the Internet Movie Database (imdb.com), Amazon, and sites like Rate Your Music (rateyourmusic.com) invite users to contribute explicit ratings, usually based on a five-star scheme, plus comments or reviews. Then there are the descriptive tags that users of MyStrands, Last.fm, and similar services can add to artists, albums, and tracks.

One of the advantages of this range of measures is that they draw on the input of a larger proportion of the audience than the minority we identified in the last chapter as Originators and Synthesizers. Though it is generally only a small proportion of people who write reviews for sites such as Amazon or the Internet Movie Database, the proportion of people contributing increases as the amount of effort required decreases. So more people are prepared to contribute simple five-star ratings and tags than detailed comments; when it comes to tracking numbers of plays, zero effort is required and everyone's preferences can be taken into account.

Having collected this fine-grained data, which is tied not just to individual files and artists but to the user who originated it as well, the sites can present it in many different ways. MyStrands and Last.fm, for example, provide you with personalized charts of your most listened-to artists and tracks (which are public so anyone can see them). The data can be sliced and diced in all manner of ways. Want to see who's popular among the Last.fm users in American Samoa? There's a chart to show you. And you can see the aggregated charts for the groups that Last.fm users have joined. Some of these groups are defined in genre terms—the Indie and Alternative group is popular, for example—but there are also thousands of people in the Born 1987 group, and you can see their charts, as well as those for members of the Deep Purple group. There are no prizes for guessing who's No. 1 for them, but the entries lower down the chart, like the band Dream Theater, act as links and recommendations for Deep Purple fans who don't yet know that band.

Last.fm provides a chart of the tags its users have given to tracks, albums, and artists, which shows something of the character of the Last.fm community: *rock*, *indie*, and *alternative* are the top three. At No. 4 is "seen live," showing how people use tags not just to classify the music itself, but also to refer to their relationship with the artists. It would be possible to provide charts for each tag, so you could check the top albums and artists for, say, *female vocalist* (Tori Amos, Björk, and Alanis Morrissette have been most frequently given this tag) or *80s* (typified by The Cure, Depeche Mode, and The Smiths). This would give you a way of browsing and exploring your interest areas through the filter of other fans' preferences. I'm told it is probably just a matter of time before such charts are available.

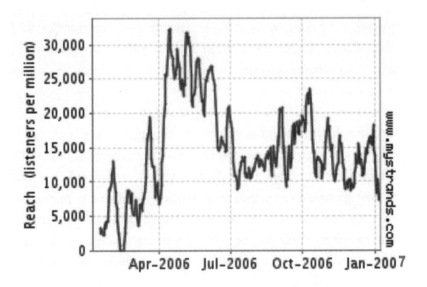

Figure 2: *Actual Reach of the Arctic Monkeys over a year, as measured by MyStrands (Copyright © MediaStrands, Inc.)*

If you want to check out who are the rising stars, go to the Artist Hype List on Last.fm, which shows which artists have seen dramatic recent increases in the number of times their songs have been listened to. Or check MyStrands' dynamic charts showing how an artist's weekly audience has grown or shrunk. MyStrands measures this with an indicator it calls the Actual Reach of an artist, defined as the number of people per million who have listened to that artist over the past seven days. Figure 2 shows how the Actual Reach of the Arctic Monkeys grew dramatically when they first burst on the scene, then fell away when the initial hype died down and began to fluctuate around an average level.

What I'd like to do is compile my own chart. I'd like to be able to select a handful of my friends with whom I share different tastes plus a few other acquaintances, critics, or DJs whom I count as tastemakers, and then see a chart aggregating what they have been listening to in the last week. Such a chart would give me useful, trusted pointers to the kind of music I might find interesting. It would also let me know when my friends and I have been listening to the same thing, which could spark further discussions. It is surely technically possible, and I hope someone will build the capability before long.

How flocking creates hits

...**In 2004 and** 2005 researchers at Columbia University in the US ran a study where they invited participants, via the web, to rate a set of songs by unknown bands. The participants were then able to download the song they had just rated—the assumption being that they would download songs they rated highly but not those that they didn't like. However, one set of participants were able to see how many times each song had already been downloaded, giving them an indication of which were the popular songs, while another set was not.[41]

When the researchers compared the ratings from these two groups, they found that the songs at the top of the download charts were generally rated as "good" by both groups, including those without access to the charts. But, statistically, those who could see the download charts tended to give higher ratings to the songs at the top of the charts. They were also more likely to download those songs themselves, which of course reinforced their high chart position in a positive feedback loop. In other words, people tended to rate songs more highly if they thought other people also liked them.

These research findings probably wouldn't come as much of a surprise to many observers of the music business, and of charts in general. In the real world beyond controlled experiments, once a song is identified as a hit, or likely hit, it gets better exposure and the media position it as "something worth listening to." (In the research study charts, the most downloaded songs similarly appeared at the top of the list, with an indication of how many downloads each had achieved.)

Clearly, this creates the potential for a kind of lock-in effect. Songs that are perceived to be highly rated by other people attract more attention, while unknown songs find it hard to get any attention, at least until people tire of those at the top of the charts and a small window of opportunity opens. But whether a new song makes it through that window, among thousands if not millions of other candidates, often appears to be a matter of luck and timing. There are many examples of songs that have been released to a fanfare of indifference and negligible sales, only to scale the top of the charts when re-released at a later date (often to coincide with some publicity phenomenon that gives extra initial momentum to the song, such as their use in an advertisement or film soundtrack). Sometimes the conditions are right for a song or film being discovered by a large number of people, and sometimes they're not.

Ratings charts and word-of-mouth opinion—like the weather—operate on nonlinear principles. There is no surefire correlation between what you put in, in the way of promotion or quality, and what you get out in terms of rewards. One of the key reasons for this nonlinearity simply comes down to the audience's scarcity of time. In the real world you don't have 48 new songs to choose from, as in the Columbia study, you have millions of them. So how do you deal with that? Do you select among them at random, or filter down your selection to just those songs that you know other people like? A seagull foraging for fish may get a bigger ration by exploring on its own, but usually following the flock is more reliable and leads more quickly to satisfaction.

However, if everyone did that all the time, new artists would find it very difficult to get a look-in. Our cultural life would be subject to a sort of mob rule, and all we would have to guide us would be an echo chamber of opinions. To complement the flocking instinct, we need some means to encourage diversity and novelty.

Separating out the cream

...Is the classic Top 40 style of chart too blunt an instrument, then, to deal with a marketplace where vastly greater ranges of audio, video, and text material are available on demand? What we need to help in discovery is something that gives people a rich indication of what other people consider to be the best material of its kind.

But how do we get a fix on what is "best"? Sales are only one crude measure, and an increasingly difficult one to aggregate when there are so many ways to consume entertainment: cinema visit, DVD rental, or download; CD, download of all or part of an album, or repeated listening on a music subscription service. When Robbie Williams' *Intensive Care* album was released in 2005, there were 164 different elements and configurations of material you could buy. These included individual tracks for music download stores, video material for a DualDisc version of the album, plus a whole set of different ringtones, screen wallpaper, and special bundles of content, some of which was exclusive to individual telecoms carriers. It's increasingly difficult for chart rules to keep up with this kind of proliferation and provide a credible measure of the overall market impact of an album package in the era of digital convergence.

Google has shown the commercial advantage of producing a genuinely useful Top 10 chart tailored to a specific interest (for that, in effect, is what the first page of its search results is). Google's "charts" are based only partly on user behavior—in particular, the site measures the number of people who have chosen to link to a web page as a sign of its popularity and relevance—with other factors being based on an analysis of the web pages themselves.

It's much harder to analyze images and sounds automatically, compared with the text on web pages. The New York-based company Platinum Blue Intelligence offers an analysis it calls Music X-Rays to predict the success of hit songs, based on the claim that many share certain musical and mathematical patterns that are not audible to the naked ear. So far, this service has been targeted at record labels and producers to help them identify the best singles and "place more intelligent investment behind songs with a better chance of market success."[42] Why not make similar technology available to all of us, so we could apply it to new releases or our old favorites and get a measure of the degree to which our own tastes are populist or anticommercial?

Flickr (www.flickr.com) is a web-based service that enables its users to upload their photographs, tag them, and share them with their friends or with the public. It provides a form of chart for photos that relies solely on different kinds of user behavior, and does not analyze the images at all. The ranking is explicitly intended to help Flickr's users discover the best among the hundreds of thousands of photos that are uploaded each day. It is called "interestingness" and it is based on a combination of measures, including how many people have viewed a photo, how many have tagged it as a favorite or in some other way, and how many have commented on it. Flickr keeps the precise algorithm for combining measures to determine interestingness under wraps—as does Google with its ranking schemes—ostensibly to guard against anyone trying to rig the rankings and promote their own work.

The recipe for producing these rankings—of web pages, songs, photographs, or other material—is both highly technical and highly sensitive. Ask any small business that has seen its website drop off the top Google search rankings when the recipe changed and it will testify to the major economic impact that the rankings have.[43] Might the same apply to albums, artists, and films in the future?

James Surowiecki's book *The Wisdom of Crowds*[44] describes several cases and circumstances where, as he puts it, the many are smarter than the few. If you ask a disparate group of people to estimate some measure or selection—Surowiecki's examples include everything from the weight of an ox to the location of a lost submarine and the contractor most culpable for the space shuttle disaster—then the average of their estimates often turns out to be more accurate than the best estimate made by an individual, even if several of the group are experts.

This effect, wherein lots of wrongs are added together and cancel each other out so they *do* make a right, seems almost like magic. It's tempting to see traces of this in Google rankings, Amazon ratings, and MySpace friends. As Surowiecki explains, however, the magic works only under certain conditions, and some of those conditions are hard to put into effect in everyday life. Perhaps most important among them are the independence and diversity of people making their assessments. It turns out to be only when your ratings are based just on your intuition and the special mix of knowledge that you bring to your assessment that the "wrongs" in your ratings effectively cancel out the "wrongs" in others' ratings. If you take much notice of what other people think, they don't cancel out any more, and everyone's ratings start to flock together in the same direction.

In the Columbia study of rating songs, one group had this independence (they had no way of finding out what other people thought when they made their ratings) and the other did not, because they could see the charts of previous ratings. This visibility of others' ratings is what Surowiecki and economists call an information cascade. Once the first decision makers have made their ratings, the later decision makers tend to use these as guidance and narrow the range of their own ratings accordingly.

There is a second factor that distinguishes ratings of audio, video, and cultural material from challenges such as estimating the weight of an ox or even predicting financial markets. You can verify the actual weight of an ox and the value of markets independently of estimates and predictions. There is no such independent measurement for cultural ratings—no "right answer" that you can use to calibrate different rating systems by determining whether this album or film is truly worth five stars or just four.

No one has yet come up with a credible composite measure of music, films, or television that combines number of plays with other indicators of value. There is no equivalent of Flickr's interestingness or Google's PageRank formula for ranking search results in these areas, at the time of writing. Creating such a measure that is both meaningful and sufficiently immune to being cheated by unscrupulous promoters is a very complex challenge. We can, however, expect further advances on the developments described above, with more finely tuned charts that help foraging fans sniff out what are the most profitable new and unknown releases for them to try out.

When it comes to supporting audiences in their discovery of interesting audio and video, our aim is to create a sufficiently reliable set of filters to give people a way of distinguishing the cream that is rising to the top from the dregs that are sinking to the bottom.

These filters may be best defined in genre and niche terms—the most popular romantic comedies from the 1940s and 1950s, or the hottest new R&B releases of the month, for instance—to help people home in on their interests. In a world where everything is available, as Chris Anderson argues in *The Long Tail*, our culture and economy become less concerned, relatively speaking, with who is king of the overall hill, and more focused on the range of artists doing well in the areas that most interest us. To encourage discovery, we are not looking for a single right answer but for a range of indicators, together with the cues and navigation to help audiences find which are useful to them.

Niches and their role as filters

...In a twist to the design of the Columbia University study, the researchers further subdivided the groups of participants who could see the download charts when they made their ratings of songs. They referred to these subdivisions as eight different "worlds" where the charts could develop independently. To what degree would these charts agree or diverge? It turned out that while there was broad similarity between many of the ratings, songs that made it to the top of the charts in one world would not always repeat this success in others (one song was No. 1 in one chart, but No. 40 out of 48 in another).

Similar effects take place in the real world, despite the global village effect of the net. The market intelligence company BigChampagne tracks the controversial area of peer-to-peer (P2P) file sharing. It can tell, region by region, which files are being shared most frequently on which P2P services. In a large territory like the US, up-and-coming bands often build a grassroots fan base in one region before they sell enough music to register on the charts. Monitoring P2P activity enables BigChampagne to predict which bands are about to cross over into large-scale success some time before they do. Furthermore, it has combined its P2P data with radio and television ratings by partnering with Nielsen Entertainment (a leading US provider of such data) to track trends and the effectiveness of different media strategies. For example, a swell of underground P2P activity on a brand-new band may create pressure for greater airplay.

Sometimes fan activity in one region spreads organically and easily into other areas. In different circumstances—in Europe, say, where there are more language and cultural barriers—this cannot be taken for granted. BigChampagne's monitoring may find that a broadcast of a promotional video in one European country is followed by increasing P2P activity for that track, but when the same video is shown in a neighboring country a few weeks later it has little or no effect.

So far, the kind of monitoring data that BigChampagne provides has been targeted mainly at the producer industries. For public relations reasons, these industries don't want to draw attention to their use of this data for market intelligence, lest it be seen in any way as an acceptance of behavior that infringes copyright. But as more P2P services are licensed and go legitimate, why not publish regional charts of activity? And why not correlate these charts not just with radio and television ratings, but also with the kinds of user playback and rating data discussed above?

With such a massive increase in the sources and volumes of data available, and the raw computing power to process and analyze it, market intelligence may become as complex and fast-changing as forecasts of the weather. Imagine a scenario:

> Clouds of Arctic Monkeys P2P activity in the north of England are building up a lot of high-pressure word of mouth, which will quickly spread across the country and could turn into a heavy precipitation of sales. Once these storms clear and sweep off west across the Atlantic, we're expecting a return to the seasonal spells of Coldplay, with occasional outbreaks of Madonna in urban areas. Scotland will continue to see a light covering of Snow Patrol.

Leaving aside the overextended metaphor, you get the idea.

So geography is not yet history in the global village. Regional variations persist and create some of the dynamics that keep things moving and keep things interesting. These variations are one of the factors that protect us from drifting toward the kind of static monoculture where the same bands, the same films, the same television commands everyone's attention month after month. Remember that one of the criteria for the wisdom of crowds effect is the independence and diversity of people making their assessments. For this to come into effect, it's helpful if people *don't* all share the same sources of information and *don't* put a lot of store by each other's ratings. As well as regional differences, country music fans mostly operate independently of R&B fans, and Savants flock in different directions to Casual fans. This brings us back to the interpretation of the Columbia University study. We avoid mob rule because these different niches of fans exist, and they forage in different ways and different areas.

The closest that an Indifferent music listener might get to rating "undiscovered" acts could be casting a vote on a television talent show like *American Idol* or *Pop Idol*. But for some Savants, scanning the scene for cutting-edge new music is part of their role. As we saw at the end of the previous chapter in the case of a young Nirvana fan, some Savants see the flock heading in one direction and consciously or instinctively head in a different direction. Most of the time the majority more or less ignores the minority, but sometimes a small group of the flock starts to peel off and follow the minority, and before you know it the whole flock has changed direction.

The increased speed of communication between fans in networked communities, combined with the greater availability (and disposability) of music and films, might mean that the spread of new favorites through fan communities becomes more volatile. If opinions about what's hot and what's not were to change direction as quickly as a school of fish, then Andy Warhol's notorious prediction that fame would last for 15 minutes could become almost literally true.

In practice, however, not even the biggest online social networks are big enough and homogeneous enough to channel this kind of influence. Social networks vary significantly in their character, and cater for different kinds of clientele doing different things. At a straightforward level, while many online music networks feature predominantly material from the major record labels, eMusic features only music from independent labels and none of the majors. Though you can make ratings and write reviews at eMusic and the iTunes Store, the main focus is on selling downloads. By contrast, the MOG social network (mog.com) does not sell music directly, it's essentially a community of music bloggers drawn together by the ability to include audio and video clips in their blog entries, as well as by each other. Reviews and ratings are a central part of the currency by which serious music fans exchange recommendations—and possibly find someone to take along as a date to the next White Stripes gig into the bargain. Even though, as we saw earlier, the top of both the Last.fm and MyStrands charts is dominated by The Beatles, Coldplay, and Red Hot Chili Peppers, it's clear if you spend much time in both environments that the ethos of each is subtly different—the norms for people interacting with each other and with the music have evolved along different lines.

Will the character of these online environments converge over time as more people join them? Those that aim for the mass market, like the iTunes Store or Amazon, probably will. But this very homogeneity will drive a sector of the market in search of alternatives with more personality and ambience, like the best private clubs or the independent stores that offer a different quality of experience from supermarkets.

The classical niche of niches

...**For an example** of a niche market that has developed outside the mainstream of popular culture and with its own traditions of discovery, consider the example of classical music. This field is perhaps typical of Long Tail trends. It comprises a very large number of catalog recordings, and is a niche made up of more niches. As Jonathan Gruber, vice-president of new media for classics and jazz at Universal Music Group International, puts it:

> There's a vast amount of (classical) repertoire and recordings, not to mention a number of different varieties of consumer interest, and it's very tough to try to pack all of that into a traditional store.[45]

Whereas classical music accounts for about 3–4% of total sales of music in shops, on the iTunes Store it accounts for 12% of sales.[46]

One of the telling features of classical music discovery is the relative lack of reliance on charts. The UK does nominally have a classical chart, but some question its status as an indicator of merit or quality. In the words of a Wikipedia contributor describing this chart, "many of the CDs sold are in fact either compilation CDs, or crossover CDs, and are not considered to be classical music by serious musicians."[47] This Wikipedian must believe either that the many are not smarter than the few when it comes to classical music, or that the issue of what should be eligible for the classical charts is contentious.

Perhaps it's a bit of both. Charts have the potential to tap the wisdom of crowds in popular culture when everyone knows a reasonable amount of what's available and they express their opinions via their purchases. Popular culture is, by definition, a mass form. Once you start to slice it into tightly defined niches, the niches no longer appeal to a broad spectrum of people. Most of the crowd are only aware of a small minority of classical releases—for reasons unrelated to the quality or merit of the others—so aggregating the crowd's opinions regarding these releases will not give the full picture.

Secondly, the categorizations involved in niches are inherently fuzzy and their demarcation is open to argument. When does an album stop being "serious" classical music and cross some invisible line to become a "crossover" album? Opinions on where to draw the line differ.

Perhaps such limitations apply to all niches. In *The Long Tail*, Chris Anderson argues that charts become more meaningful, and more useful as filters to guide our explorations, when they are aggregated at a niche or genre level. His argument is that when the items in a chart are more similar—the example he uses is Afro-Cuban jazz artists—the comparison between their popularity is a more meaningful measure of what might be worth checking out. The question is: What is an appropriate level of definition for the charts and is it the same for everyone? Can we go further and divide the Afro-Cuban jazz charts into salsa charts, merengue charts, and so on? Such classifications may be a useful aid for some foraging and exploration, but the more tightly you define the niches, the more knowledge and expertise you require from foragers to navigate these distinctions. How many of us can reliably distinguish even between Afro-Cuban jazz and other forms of Latin jazz?

So if charts are of only limited use, how *do* people find out what others like and discover classical music? The answer seems to be that they use multiple methods, searching, browsing, and monitoring multiple sources of information. With any genre outside the vernacular forms of popular culture, you also have to commit considerable time to extended and concentrated listening to give your ears time to attune themselves to nuances that are not revealed immediately. Frequently this also involves guided listening, when a friend or a teacher plays a piece of music for you and points out important features.

Over the centuries, classical music practitioners have developed a wide range of resources to support this process of extended exploration and acculturation. We are now starting to see that range replicated, at a much faster pace, for other niche areas of our culture, where aficionados are recording and sharing their learning experiences via the net.

An active and growing fan economy involves a thriving community passing recommendations, making links, and generating data in the form of charts, tags, and listening or viewing patterns. Perhaps the classical music field shows what happens to a fan economy as it matures. Its terminology and values become more established and entrenched. It becomes institutionalized, and listeners come to rely relatively more on professionals and less on fellow fans. That's part of the reason why classical music is not rock 'n' roll. In the next part of the book we look at the changing role of professionals and how they may be able to make discovery work better.

Part III
Tapping the experts

5

Who knows?...

etween 2005 and 2006, eMusic expanded its staff of editorial contributors to 120. The new recruits included high-profile names such as the producer and compiler (and member of the Patti Smith Group) Lenny Kaye, celebrated comic-book writer Harvey Pekar (subject of the film *American Splendor*), and widely respected music journalist Simon Reynolds. During this period eMusic had emerged as the second most successful licensed music download service, behind Apple's iTunes Store, despite the fact that it does not include any music from major record labels, which rules out the majority of big-hit artists.

Apple achieved its dominant position with a smaller editorial staff. And the independent music featured on eMusic attracts some of the most articulate and committed bloggers, who write their own reviews and make them freely available. So when Apple has a skeleton staff for its music service and other services like MySpace and Last.fm rely extensively on contributions made by their users, what is eMusic doing investing in editors? Has it lost the plot?

The answer is that eMusic is one of several players who are redefining the role of editors, and of intermediaries in the media more generally. eMusic is not playing quite the same game as Apple. The iTunes Store has achieved its billions of downloads by selling moderate numbers of tracks (on average) to large numbers of people. In contrast, eMusic aims to sell larger numbers of tracks, from a smaller catalog, to a smaller and more specialist market. Its payment model encourages this behavior by requiring a fixed monthly payment, in return for between 30 and 75 downloaded tracks per month. The editors' reviews, selections, and magazine are designed to attract and guide you to music that you don't yet know. In other words, eMusic depends on discovery. By comparison, the iTunes Store is, so far, more geared to customers who already know what they want when they arrive at the store, search for it, download it, and then move on.

Media power: Spreading it all about

...In the early days of opening the internet to large-scale commerce, some predicted that it would spell the end of intermediaries: that each of us listeners, viewers, readers, and players would communicate directly with the producers of the stuff we were interested in. But instead of disappearing, most intermediaries have in fact adapted, albeit fairly radically, and often involving a shift onto the net.

Hence examples like eMusic and the All Media Guide, which, as well as publishing its own allmusic, allmovie, and allgames guides, also licenses its information and its software to others, including eMusic (and, indeed, iTunes). On eMusic's site, reviews from allmusic sit alongside those by in-house reviewers, because not even 120 editorial staff can review everything in the catalog. This is an example of the new generation of intermediaries that has emerged to help us find our way through the enormous volume of stuff available to keep us entertained.

The question is not whether we need intermediaries, but what kind of intermediaries they should be, and how best to run them. As we've seen, the All Media Guide is editor led in the old-school style where qualified professionals take responsibility for guiding us through terrain that they know better than us. But is the clock ticking for this model, as more and more recommendations are generated by software algorithms, and commentary is increasingly contributed by fans via blogs and wikis?

Zac Johnson, who has been at All Media Guide since 2000 working particularly on allmusic, is at the sharp end of this question. But if he's worried about technology and blog culture taking his job away, he wasn't showing any signs of it when I spoke to him. Johnson recognizes that the recommendations generated by software code and by social filtering can be useful. The "intelligent playlisting" technologies he's developing for licensing to allmusic's customers aim to take advantage of such methods where they can. But the methods have limitations for which editorial input can compensate.

Take collaborative filtering, for example. Collaborative filtering, as we saw in Chapter 1, is what underpins recommendations made by Last.fm when putting together a personalized radio station, or those made by Amazon when suggesting further purchases based on your recent ones. The recommendations you receive are based on the behavior of other consumers who share at least some of your tastes.

As Johnson explains, this means that collaborative filtering tends to reinforce popular and established patterns of preference, at the expense of exposing new or less widely appreciated music. So, for example, if you say you like The Beatles, you may be recommended Bob Marley or James Brown, because they are all very popular artists and many people like all three. Conversely, you're unlikely to be recommended the new album by Baaba Maal, because not many people have heard it yet and so far it has appealed only to a modest audience.

Johnson believes that by augmenting collaborative filtering with some editorial input, it becomes possible to open up what he calls the "tastemaker" end of the spectrum. This could involve providing recommendations for new music (or films, games, or books) that is just starting to attract a following or, as we will see later, suggesting older material that may have been forgotten or overlooked when it was first released.

We'll explore the pros and cons of editorial interventions in a moment, but the first and most important trend of recent years in this area is the dilution of the authority associated with editors and intermediaries. For most of the twentieth century, there were hoops you had to jump through to raise awareness of a song or a film. The number of intermediaries—television or radio networks, press reviews, retail or exhibition chains—was limited. As a result, intermediaries wielded considerable influence through their editorial decisions. In his comprehensive history of the record industry, *Where Have All the Good Times Gone?*,[48] Louis Barfe describes the stranglehold exerted on US major labels right up to the 1980s by an affiliation of independent promotion men known as "the Network." These radio and television pluggers were able to resist attempts to get round their cartel by proving conclusively that they could make or break a record. They were gatekeepers in the sense that they had the power to decide who did and did not pass along to the next stage in gaining exposure to a large audience. Leading DJs, influential magazines like *Rolling Stone*, and later MTV also wielded considerable gatekeeper power.

Now a different kind of network is in play. Reflecting the architecture of the internet itself, no one enjoys the same degree of gatekeeper control over what gets seen and what gets heard. If promotional efforts come up against a brick wall, they simply route round it and find another way to reach their target audience. From the other end, if fans don't find the kind of material they want through mainstream media channels, they simply switch their attention to niche media that do cater to those interests.

Of course, it still helps if you can persuade the editor of the iTunes Store to feature your new release on its main page, if eMusic's staff give it a good review, or if allmusic bumps it into its intelligent playlisting service as a potential Next Big Thing. But in each case the editorial staff concerned know that their role is a facilitating one, not a controlling one.

This shift in the distribution of power is by no means unique to the discovery and retailing of entertainment. It's a by-product of the way the net is designed that even though the Amazons, eBays, and Googles of the world may achieve pre-eminent market share, no one has final and exclusive authority. As a customer, user, fan, or whatever, you always have alternatives. This fundamental fact has far-reaching implications that are manifest in shifts in the way things are done in several domains. As the learning and training field has moved online, for example, there is an equivalent loss of authority for teachers and instructors. Instead of being the "sage on the stage" who controls the flow of information to learners, they become the "guide on the side" who facilitates self-motivated exploration and reflection on the fruits of that exploration.

As for educators, so for editors. Their challenge in the digital discovery era is to create a "patch" that keeps you coming back and encourages you to forage there for new material. It should ideally include opportunities for each of the TLC strands: to try out material, follow links, and exchange recommendations with peers. To understand the nature of this challenge, let's first look at what can be achieved *without* editors, curators, librarians, or professionals of any kind.

Imagine no professionals

...Martin Stiksel, co-founder of Last.fm, explains how the site set out with a policy of no editors. Last.fm is still an intermediary between music producers and listeners, but its policy means that it doesn't intervene to promote any artist or track (as a general rule; modest exceptions will be mentioned later). Instead, it has built a forum or platform to allow fans to try out, organize, discuss, and recommend a wide range of music. What happens next is up to the fans. The depth and breadth of what each of them explores on Last.fm have developed organically based on what all of them do and what they contribute.

How do you build a platform that enables a diverse wealth of information, filters, and recommendations to emerge spontaneously? Last.fm demonstrates several of the necessary components: personalized listening, user-generated content, folksonomies, interactive charts, and other features to build community. These cross the professional domains of, variously, the DJ, the musicologist, the journalist, and the librarian.

Democratize the DJ

Personalized trying out comes from Last.fm's collaborative filtering technology. Effectively this plays the role of a disc jockey in devising the playlist of tracks you hear. One difference is that the Last.fm recommendation engine is interactive. If you don't like a track, you can say so and it is replaced immediately. The engine remembers what you say you love and hate, and tailors its playlists to take these into account. Another difference, which some may construe as an advantage, is the lack of DJ chatter (and advertising) between songs.

Every time you tell Last.fm about your preferences, this refines the associative links listed under the "Similar to" tab for each artist, reinforcing the links between artists whom most users have in common. It is important to remember that this harvesting of data from listening behavior does not demand hard work on the part of the listener; it does not require you to think about how your actions might influence others. You just have to focus on what you, selfishly, want to hear. Last.fm does all the hard graft, acting as a kind of distilling plant, mixing the by-products of your choices with those of others. The result of this distillation is a rich network of associative links, similar in appearance to the kind of mapping of musical patterns and relationships that (as we will see in the next chapter) expert musicologists spend their lives refining.

What is more—and this is a key point that will recur several times in the book—the more people use Last.fm, the richer and more reliable that network becomes. The more selfish choices by more people you add together, the greater the collective wealth you realize. Building this wealth from huge numbers of individually tiny contributions is known as "crowdsourcing."

DIY journalism

Aside from these implicit contributions, Last.fm encourages any more explicit commentary and material that you might feel like sharing with other users. It has descriptive profiles for artists and record labels that operate as wikis, so that any user can edit them at any time. While only a minority of users will actually do this, it's likely to be those who are most articulate and knowledgeable (about the area in question) who volunteer such contributions. If being a big Radiohead fan is an important part of your identity, what better way to demonstrate it than to be first to update the band's profile with news of a solo album by one of its members, thus gaining kudos among fellow fans?

Perhaps, however, I am also a Radiohead fan and when I come to view the band's profile I think the news of the solo album could be more accurately or more eloquently described. I change what you have written (after all, I have my own kudos to consider). Again, the more fans who use the system, the more likely it is that inaccuracies will be ironed out and expression will be improved. In the process, of course, you have substituted for the role of a professional journalist, while I, and the fans who follow me in making changes, are doing the work of subeditors.

Keeping it classified

One of the challenges of presenting a catalog for users to browse—whether it's for music, books, films and videos, games, or photographs—is working out which categories to use. Take a film like *The Big Lebowski*, for example. Imagine you want to help a casual browser discover this film, when she's unsure of exactly what she wants except that it should be exciting and funny. Should you give her the option of finding it under Comedy or Thrillers, and also under a second-level heading of Comedy Thrillers? What if Thriller wasn't quite the term she associates with exciting? The Internet Movie Database has the film classified as Comedy, Crime, and Mystery. Wikipedia has it as Black Comedy, Cult Films, and Neo-Noir. Allmovie has it as Comedy, Crime Comedy, Screwball Comedy, and Buddy Film. These are all accurate classifications. Librarians and other specialists are trained in devising and managing them. But are they the terms that the potential audience for the film has in mind when they arrive at a website?

As we saw in Chapter 1, folksonomies are a way of letting amateurs make up and assign their own classification terms as tags. Using these folksonomy tags means that Last.fm does not have to try to second-guess what terms its users will find most useful; it lets them specify. When allmusic describes the moods of the Pet Shop Boys' music variously as *bittersweet*, *campy*, *dramatic*, *restrained*, *exuberant*, and *detached*, it has to have fairly clear definitions of those terms to ensure they are applied in a consistent way (for example, Nina Simone is another *bittersweet* artist and Joni Mitchell's *Blue* is a *bittersweet* album, while Elliott Smith is *restrained*).

No one on Last.fm consults anyone else about definitions before they apply a tag; they just do it. So don't expect consistency when comparing one person's use of tags with another's. However, if you aggregate everyone's tags, the more eccentric and erratic uses get drowned out, and you are left with a set of classifications that turn out to be fairly robust. (Remember that it's music we're classifying here, not hazardous chemicals or aircraft pilots, so 99.9% accuracy is neither expected nor required.)

Showing that the Last.fm amateurs agree with allmusic professionals at least part of the time, Elliott Smith turns out to be the artist most frequently tagged as *restrained*. There are no artists, albums, or tracks that have been tagged as *detached* more than three times, at the time of writing, so searching Last.fm using this term will not get reliable results. Then again, the more people who use the service, the more developed and refined the usefulness of each term will become.

Amateur motivations

It's an obvious point but, if you're going to depend on unpaid volunteers to create, categorize, and manage your content, then you had better make sure there's something in it for them. In the case of Wikipedia and writing profiles, the incentive might be the sense of pride and achievement that comes from contributing to the collective store of knowledge. For most of the people, most of the time, you need a payoff that is more immediately fun and engaging. This is where Last.fm—along with MySpace, MyStrands, and a growing number of entertainment sites—have taken a leaf from the book of the early social networking sites, ranging from the WELL to Friendster.

The key is to make listening to music, watching films, or reading books into social activities once more—the kinds of things you do with a view to chatting about them with your friends, making new friends with similar interests, comparing and recommending favorites, and perhaps even gaining status as an opinion leader.

The WELL (www.well.com), now one of the world's longest-established online communities, started as a dial-up bulletin board system in the San Francisco Bay area in the 1980s, when there was no prospect of online music or video to attract users. Everything was text. But it attracted amateur and professional writers with offers of free accounts in return for their contributions. When the likes of MySpace, Last.fm, and MyStrands invite independent and unsigned artists to contribute their music, they are doing the same thing: ensuring a steady stream of new material to attract other users. MySpace currently claims almost as many recording artists on its site as the iTunes Store has tracks.[49] The artists add further juice to the mix because they are motivated, in terms of self-promotion, to encourage people to visit the sites and see or hear their material.

With the help of this kind of kick-start, Last.fm and its ilk have been able to draw growing numbers of fans into the experience of exploring new material and then tagging it, listing it, and discussing it with each other. The key to any social network platform is to keep the flow of new material and discussion going. The combination of entertainment content and fan involvement promises to be more sustainable than either element would be on its own.

What motivates ordinary users to spend time updating wikis or tagging content? A group of researchers affiliated with Yahoo! investigated this in connection with tagging on some of the services that Yahoo! owns. They found that a mix of selfish and social incentives comes into play. We add tags to things to help us find them later, to help share them with others, to draw others' attention to them, to express opinions about them, and to manage the way other people see us.[50]

The limitations of bottom-up

...If user-driven, bottom-up services such as Last.fm can evolve and develop under their own steam, they will challenge the status quo in the media industries. By radically reducing editorial costs, their model could prove disruptive. Unsurprisingly, there are doubts and criticisms from several quarters, including from the professionals whose hard-won expertise, through qualifications and long apprenticeships, seems to be devalued. In *The Cult of the Amateur*,[51] Andrew Keen worries that the sheer volume of blogs could corrupt and confuse popular opinion about everything from politics and commerce to arts and culture. He believes that kids can't tell the difference between "credible news by objective professional journalists" and the work of bloggers.

So how reliable is the information you glean from a blog, a wiki, or a user forum? Well, it varies. It varies in the same way that day-to-day conversations do, from the expert expressing an opinion at work that she knows will be scrutinized by colleagues, through to the barstool provocateur shooting opinions from the hip purely for the sake of argument. If you have to stake your life or your reputation on something, you would be best advised to consult a long-established publication, one whose reputation has been honed and trustworthiness tested over many years. No one should be complacent about the risks of popular opinion being corrupted, but there are at least two reasons to believe that the risks in the area of cultural discovery are only modest.

First, we can acknowledge the variability of blogs and the fluidity of wikis, yet it seems that as we become more familiar with these forms, we become better at judging the ways in which their reliability varies. If you see a wiki-based artist profile that has one or two incomplete sentences, and makes sweeping statements about which albums are good and which are rubbish, then this may prompt you to check the "version history" of what you're reading. If you see that the profile was created two weeks ago and only two people have contributed to it, then you would be justified in being skeptical about what the profile says. If, on the other hand, you see another profile that has been laid out with subheadings, images, and references to other sources, all of which clearly reflect the house style for profiles, it's a fairly safe bet that the information has been researched, reviewed by many eyes, and polished by many hands. You can feel correspondingly safer in trusting what you read. Over time, progressively greater scrutiny starts to sort out the reliable wikis and blogs from the fly-by-night ones—and kids, having grown up with these new media forms, may be particularly adept at making such distinctions.

A second point, already touched on, is that the kind of information you find on the likes of Last.fm and MySpace typically isn't the kind on which lives depend. If public opinion about last night's Elton John concert is confused, the worst that will happen is a few people will regret choosing to attend tonight's concert. Elton will be pleased to be talked about in any way. Indeed, in much of the entertainment media, gossip, speculation, and opinion have greater currency than cross-checked facts. In this field, one role of journalists is to keep their finger on the pulse of the fans, and to catch the buzz of a breaking artist or film before other media channels do. With Last.fm and MySpace more people can be part of the buzz, rather than hearing about it later.

Notwithstanding these defenses, it is too early to demarcate the limits of user-driven techniques like wikis and folksonomies. A large part of the success of Wikipedia is precisely that, by being the first endeavor of its kind, it has attracted both attention and authority. If I know that my contributions are going into the world's pre-eminent free online encyclopedia and may be read by hundreds of thousands of people in my area of knowledge, I will be motivated and on top of my game. If, on the other hand, there were several wikis with competing interests and large areas of overlap, I might think twice.

That's where the initial success and profile of Wikipedia work to its advantage. It's going to be very difficult for anyone to initiate from scratch a free wiki-based online encyclopedia to compete with Wikipedia in the near future; there can be only one. In the music domain, on the other hand, Last.fm has its wiki profiles, and new user-driven resources like the Wiki Music Guide and Napster's Narchive (styled "the people's music archive") were launched in 2006. It is hard to see any of these, which overlap with the commercial service provided by allmusic and its competitors, becoming pre-eminent in the way that Wikipedia has. Perhaps some of them could end up licensing their material from Wikipedia itself, which, of course, has its own extensive artist (and album) profiles.

As well as bringing advantages, the high profile of Wikipedia produces pressures of its own. The greater the store that users put in Wikipedia (or any similar enterprise with user input), the greater the incentive for unscrupulous people to try to game them by distorting the information. This creates problems of governance—how to manage persistent "offenses" while retaining the openness that created the conditions for success in the first place.

Similar issues are likely to arise in folksonomies as well. To say that we don't know how well folksonomy tagging systems will scale up may sound churlish in the light of the many millions of web-page bookmarks that have been tagged using social book-marking services like del.icio.us and the millions of photographs tagged in Flickr's photo-sharing service. However, on the global scale of the internet, del.icio.us and Flickr are the equivalent of the early social gatherings, the first villages, as net users become less isolated in their online behavior and start to coordinate with each other, finding places to settle. As Matt Locke, commissioning editor for education and new media at Channel 4, writes:

> The dirt paths have a habit of becoming roads, and border towns turn into cities, and suddenly we're having to think about governance, authority, access, and representation again. This hasn't happened yet with many folksonomy projects, but it will.[52]

This metaphor captures another of the challenges that will face bottom-up media. While the new social gathering places are growing and developing, everyone involved is excited. The participants see the opportunity to make their name, or, perhaps, their fortune. As the villages grow to become towns and then cities, there's a risk that some will become more jaded, more alienated. Will this create a need for a new breed of professionals to manage the regeneration and police the disaffected users?

With so many gates, who needs keepers?

...In 2006, *Wired News* reporter Ryan Singel filed a 1,000-word story on how wikis are being used. His editor suggested it would be an interesting exercise to make the draft article available for a week as a wiki page to be edited by readers. At the end of the week, the article was 60% longer. It was, in Singel's opinion, more accurate and representative. But, he argued, it had lost some of the narrative flow of the original, the transitions were "choppy," and there was too much dry explication.[53] Singel didn't make this comparison explicit, but his piece had become more like an encyclopedia entry.

Some might argue that these criticisms are clinging on to outmoded and hidebound professional values. It's not unusual for the roles of professionals—including journalists and editors—to shift from time to time. One possibility would be to leave them to do the tidying up after the newly empowered but undisciplined fans have had their say. But the history of new technology suggests this would not be a rewarding solution for anyone.

The role of media gatekeeper has gone for good. The days of unquestioned authority enjoyed by a cadre of professional critics are over; even highbrow newspapers supplement reviews by their most esteemed film critics with a selection of "vox pop" opinions about the same films from apparently random members of the public. Three options remain for professional critics: go with the flow; resist and aim to stand out from the crowd; or find some accommodation that encourages dialog, participation, and is closer to the "guide on the side" ethos.

Go with the flow

Creating lists is one example of going with the flow. Online and offline media are bursting with lists of every size and shape; everyone loves a list, remember, to help to make sense of the awesome nature and volume of material available to us. There is a website (listsofbests.com) that offers several lists of "best of" lists. But if professional journalists and program makers just conjure up their own lists, they are doing exactly the same as any blogger could do; one of the appeals of lists is that anyone can make one. So the value the professionals add is in their more established distribution and readership, and an occasionally questionable claim to greater discernment in their compilations. Is this a sustainable long-term future for the mainstream media? It's more likely that the "anyone can do that" factor will undermine the value that people attach to these media.

Stand out from the crowd

The second option is to stick it out by relying wholly on the core professional skills that, as Ryan Singel implies, are not widely spread across the population: telling stories, marshaling arguments, and keeping their cultural antennae tuned to the trends that the rest of us haven't quite articulated yet (even if we're living in the middle of them).

To carry this off with authority, it helps to be a star turn or a well-established media brand. Martin Scorsese's *No Direction Home* story of Bob Dylan's early career won great acclaim and sales in its own right, and also prompted a tenfold increase in sales of Dylan's older albums in the wake of its broadcast and DVD release.[54] The BBC has produced a massive catalog of music documentaries for radio, from star profiles (including, for example, a 10-hour series on John Lennon) to features on celebrated music venues and record labels (such as the 14-hour *Story of Atlantic Records*, which includes an extraordinary range of exclusive interviews).

Star producers and mainstream media are not the whole of the story, however. On a smaller scale, independent documentary films and books about the life stories of cult artists (Nick Drake, Daniel Johnston, Jonathan Richman) do much to bring their work to a larger audience and develop the interests of casual fans. The producers of these films and authors of these books are frequently, like bloggers, self-commissioned. The difference is that they have accepted the disciplines of longer forms (careful structuring and holding attention) and the generally higher production costs involved. And if costs are greater, so is the pressure to get a return by reaching a larger audience.

Even the web has some professional publications that have held out, so far, against encouraging direct participation by their intended audience. The Pitchfork music site (www.pitchforkmedia.com) aims to fulfill the old-fashioned roles of tastemaker and filter for independent and "alternative" music. It styles itself as the "home of the gratuitously in-depth record review," and record reviews, along with news items and features, are what it delivers—without user comments, ratings, or tags. At the time of writing, Pitchfork continues to carry this off with some aplomb and influence. It holds a position of genuine authority among its target market, based solely on its track record of being close to the action and describing it well.

Guide on the side

There's a compromise approach that imaginatively blends elements of blog culture and the mainstream media, thus developing a dialog between those media and their audience. The UK's *Guardian* newspaper has a weekly feature in which the journalist Dorian Lynskey solicits playlist suggestions from readers on the newspaper's culture blog. Each playlist has a theme that prompts readers to think about the music they know in a possibly unusual way: the top ten songs about London, about one-night stands, short songs, songs with "song" in the title, and so on.[55] After a few days, Lynskey calls a halt to the suggestions and then publishes his selection of ten, with commentary, in the newspaper (the "long list" remains accessible online on the blog). In this way, his playlist draws on a wider pool of expertise than any one person could command on their own, while the published article retains a consistent individual perspective.

Through this semi-participative approach, the mainstream media are not emulating blogs *per se*, they are emulating the kind of *platform* that Last.fm and Wikipedia provide, with the added value of professional input. If the wiki model is like putting a bunch of people around a table with a blank sheet of paper and just leaving them to get on with it, then *The Guardian*'s weekly playlist is like giving these people a professional facilitator to guide the conversation, solicit contributions, and then provide a tidy record of proceedings at the end.

The symbiosis between pro and amateur is not limited simply to the mainstream media, but can apply to supporting discovery in niche areas. Providing such support requires sensitivity to the gap between what most people can do for themselves and the less obvious features of an area. At the start of this decade, I held a board position at an independent cinema and helped provide web-based resources to support the specialist seasons of films that were shown. For example, we ran a series of films by the Italian director Luchino Visconti. Anyone could type Visconti's name into their favorite search engine and retrieve a reasonable list of useful sites. Part of my task was to short-circuit some of the further foraging that film fans would have to do from there: to sift a range of reviews of the films that were showing in the season, and to get a balance between biographical information and critical appreciation. Beyond that I also knew that a couple of Visconti's films are set during the Risorgimento, a period of nineteenth-century Italian history with which few of the audience were likely to be familiar. Nor, it seemed to me at the time, was it likely that they would find their way to this historical context if left to their own devices. So among the web resources, I included a link to a brief overview of this period, to provide background information for viewing and fully understanding the films.

The three options—going with the flow, standing out from the crowd, or guiding from the side—are not mutually exclusive, and free-range foraging fans will draw on all of them. Smart professionals and amateurs have already moved on and are learning to find an accommodation with each other that offers the best of all worlds.

Rediscovering lost classics

...So what are these amateur and professional resources for? To help us find a way to new areas we wouldn't uncover otherwise. We need reviews, DJs, classifications, and stories to filter and render digestible the overwhelming mountain of material—whether music, video, text, or other media—that fills our world. In previous generations, the market disciplines of physical distribution did a considerable amount of filtering for us. With only a finite amount of shelf space in stores and finite airtime on limited radio and television networks, it only made sense to distribute stuff that significant numbers of people were interested in.

As well as the tastes we share with many others, most of us have some more idiosyncratic and minority tastes that local

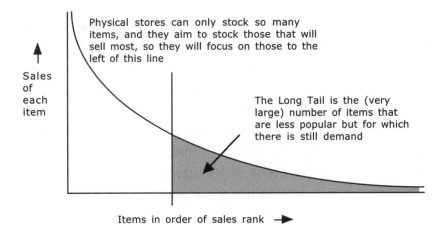

Figure 3 *The Long Tail*

stores do not cater for. If digital distribution overcomes the limitations of shelf space, will we shift our attention toward more of those marginal interests and away from the hits that everyone enjoys? That's the thesis that Chris Anderson explores and expounds in *The Long Tail*. As a digitally powered business strategy, the Long Tail is about exploiting the untapped demand that lies outside the mainstream. The "tail" is the part of a sales distribution where sales are lower, but where there is a very large number of items (see Figure 3). If you can find a cost-effective way of connecting each of the items in the tail with the people who are interested in them, then you have yourself a business opportunity. The sum of lots of small demand turns out to represent quite significant revenues.

Anderson's key finding from his research with online businesses like Rhapsody for digital music tracks and Netflix for DVDs is that the tail turns out to be very long indeed. You have to go very far down the tail before you reach items for which there is no demand.

The Long Tail does not mean the end of big hits, but intuitively it makes sense of what we perceive as the increased visibility of vintage films, old music, and minority-taste material from beyond the current charts. In the limitless shelf space of the iTunes Store, for example, niche music accounts for a significantly higher percentage of sales than it does in physical retail outlets. Digital storage also compresses shelf space at home, enabling fans to build ever-larger collections, and thus they are demanding a broader range of material.

One of the things that hampers the material in the Long Tail, however, is the neglect that it has suffered, which makes it hard for even interested fans to find. DJs haven't played it, stores haven't stocked it, no one has classified it, reviewed it, or written interview features about it. Perhaps, you think, that was for good reason. How detailed a review do you need to reach the conclusion "It's crap"? But remember that a lot of Long Tail material has its defenders, and in some cases the mix of bottom-up discovery and professional assessment can discover, or rediscover, lost gems and give them a lift from the tail toward the head.

In fact, this is one of the effects that Anderson cited when first reporting the phenomenon, telling the story of Joe Simpson's book *Touching the Void*, which did only modest business when first published but then became a bestseller ten years later.[56] In this case, the new lease of life was sparked by Amazon's automated recommendation system, which drew customers' attention to the fact that some buyers of a new, popular mountain-climbing book had also bought *Touching the Void*. After this stimulated sales a little, word-of-mouth recommendations and increasing media awareness did the rest. A snowball effect was created that led to the book becoming a bestseller and ultimately being turned into a film.

A similar rediscovery from the music world shows the power of the combination of grassroots processes and professional media. Vashti Bunyan's 1970 album *Just Another Diamond Day* was, like *Touching the Void*, a commercial failure on its initial release; only a few hundred copies were pressed.

Vashti left the music business shortly afterward and more or less forgot the album for over a quarter of a century. However, the small number of remaining vinyl copies became increasingly treasured items among a new generation of folk fans, many of them in America. With its ears close enough to the ground to detect this following, heritage music magazine *Mojo* featured *Just Another Diamond Day* in its regular obscurities column called "Buried Treasure." This, together with the prices the record was commanding on eBay, gave Vashti Bunyan the confidence to press for, and secure, a CD reissue of the album in 2000. When this was greeted with rave reviews and fueled support for her among young folk performers, she was invited to play live for the first time in decades. She then wrote and recorded a follow-up album, *Lookaftering*, released 35 years after its predecessor, again to a warm welcome and multiple features and interviews in the media.

Vashti Bunyan is by no means unique in being granted a second performing career later in life (she is 61). The Cuban musicians featured in the Buena Vista Social Club were even older when they found a mass audience outside their native island—an audience whose demand for this brand of Cuban rhythms had been latent. In this case, the early spark seemed to be generated by professionals who could trade on their reputations. The *Buena Vista Social Club* album was produced by the renowned guitarist Ry Cooder, and award-winning director Wim Wenders made a documentary about the performers. It was with the help of that initial push that word-of-mouth recommendations took over and the music started to rise up from the tail.

At the end of *The Long Tail*, Anderson says:

> The secret to creating a thriving Long Tail business can be summarized in two imperatives: 1. Make everything available; 2. Help me find it.

Not everyone in the Long Tail can count on the equivalents of *Mojo* magazine, Ry Cooder, and Wim Wenders to help people find their material. When we consider that the number of music tracks runs into the tens of millions and that of films into hundreds of thousands, it becomes clear that there's a need to explore methods that can scale to cope with these vast amounts of material.

When we're trying to devise ways to help people find stuff, it's useful to analyze what it is about the stuff that they like. So the next chapter reviews different approaches that have been taken to analyzing music and video, using human skill and computer power to match it to our tastes and activities.

6

Cracking the code of content...

In 1960 the pioneering American folklorist Alan Lomax began what may not have been the first, but was certainly among the most ambitious attempts to create a framework to code and analyze the world's music. Over nearly four decades, he worked on a coding system he called "cantometrics"—literally, "the measure of song."

With his assistant, Lomax reviewed 700 recordings from 250 cultural areas of the world. Reflecting the state of the art at the time, none of the 37 cantometric scales could have more than 13 values, as that was the maximum number of columns on the IBM punchcards they were using for data processing. With these scales, Lomax was able to map clusters of musical forms and speculate about their development through history. For example, he showed how the song styles of Pygmies and Bushmen were almost identical (though they lived 3,000 miles apart in very different environments), except that the Bushmen also had a solo "blues" tradition, reflecting their different courtship circumstances. He showed that some western European contrapuntal music shared some characteristics with Pygmy–Bushman forms, but that apart from this, European traditions were significantly different. The principal pattern of European folk song involved, Lomax determined, a leader dominating a passive audience, rather than the more participative model of the Pygmy–Bushman style.

Global Jukebox

...**As this example** hints, Alan Lomax did not treat music as simply entertainment. He believed that music embodied the very soul of the people who made and listened to it. Lomax saw cantometrics as a way to use songs as a measure of both song and society, and also developed measures of dance ("choreometrics") as part of a wider anthropological mapping of global cultures. His liberal progressive agenda drove Lomax toward educational goals. When multimedia technologies started to become available in the late 1970s, he saw their potential to realize a system he called the "Global Jukebox." This would make all his mappings available through an attractive and easy-to-use interface, so that everyone would be able to discover their own cultural roots, learn how their area of the world fitted into the global picture, and trace some of the connections between cultures.[57]

It's hard to overstate the reach of Alan Lomax's vision. He saw sound and movement—rather than oral or written language—as the deep structure of our identities. Through his collecting, notating, and interpretation, he sought to chart the ways in which we are different from each other, and the ways in which we are the same.

At one point, the Global Jukebox received support from Apple and the US National Science Foundation, among others, and a prototype system was built in the 1990s. However, Lomax failed to win over the academic community. Some argued that the important features of musical culture could not be abstracted into lists of traits like the 37 cantometric scales. Academics criticized the scales themselves for being imprecise, as well as Lomax's application of them, which relied exclusively on North American judges and—many felt—excluded features that did not yield the results he wanted.[58] By the mid-1990s funders withdrew their support, and Alan Lomax, now an octogenarian, could no longer proceed with the project. Thus one man's enormously ambitious vision to map the music of the world, along with its connections to our experience and relationships, came to an end.

Music Genome

...The story of music analysis does not stop there, though. The Music Genome Project's name reflects the fact that it was conceived in a different era—the twenty-first century—and perhaps with a more biological understanding of music in mind. However, this is not an initiative that aims to unravel the DNA of music just for the sake of enriching our cultural understanding.

The Music Genome Project is a commercial venture. Like cantometrics, it is based on a list of traits assessed by trained analysts who listen to songs and record their traits on a set of scales. Compared with Lomax's 700 recordings, the Music Genome Project has so far classified over half a million, with more being added all the time.[59] Yet, so far, these come from a smaller gene pool than Lomax's, being mostly western pop and rock from the past 50 years.

Instead of applying its analysis to general cross-cultural education, as with the Global Jukebox, the main application of the Music Genome Project to date is to recommend to its users music that they don't yet know but may wish to buy. You can access this through an online music service called Pandora (www.pandora.com). You enter the names of one or more artists you like into Pandora and, based on the analysis of the "genetic" make-up of songs by these artists, the service plays you more songs with similar sets of "genes" (Pandora itself doesn't refer to these as genes; I am just extending the genome metaphor).

Pandora is thus very similar to Last.fm in providing a kind of personalized radio station. As with Last.fm, you can also "train" Pandora by letting it know if you particularly like, or dislike, any of the tracks it plays you. Many music fan bloggers have tried the two services under similar conditions, and have shared their opinions on how the quality of the recommendations and the user experience compares between the two.[60]

Although the inputs and outputs of Last.fm and Pandora are of the same kind, the process by which they generate their outputs from inputs is quite different. Last.fm's processing, as we saw in Chapter 1, is agnostic about the qualities of the music itself, simply saying, "Here are some tracks that other people with a similar listening profile to yours seem to like." But the Music Genome element of Pandora says, "Here are some tracks that have a similar musical profile to the ones you like."

What do we know about the traits that make up these musical profiles? Because the scales and framework of the Music Genome Project are proprietary and intended to be used for commercial advantage, they are not published and available for scrutiny by other musicologists in the same way that Alan Lomax's cantometrics were. Nevertheless, a few basic details can be established. At the basic level, the Music Genome Project classifies music into one of four genres: rock/pop/country; jazz; hip-hop/electronic; and world music (hence my earlier comment about the skew toward western music). Beyond that, you can ask Pandora why it recommended a particular track and it will specify the traits (or genes) that underpinned its recommendation. These include elements like "electronica roots," "use of modal harmonies," "a unique harmonic progression," "emphasis on instrumental performance," "atmospheric production," "extensive vamping," "minor key tonality," and "an electric guitar solo."[61]

Genetic codes and musical relationships

...**The reason the** formulations of Alan Lomax and the Music Genome Project are important to digital discovery is that they imply there is an underlying structure to music and possibly an equivalent underlying structure to our tastes and preferences. If this proved to be the case, it could have profound implications for the discovery process. By analyzing everything from the latest new releases to Long Tail obscurities, we could filter out all the stuff that won't appeal to you, leaving just the essence that will. You need forage and explore no more—we can provide you with a scientifically proven optimum and personalized diet that you're almost guaranteed to like.

So, whether or not experts might argue about the precise definition of the genres and genes, is there really a genetic code out of which all music is made? Or does the criticism leveled at cantometrics—that some important features of music do not lend themselves to abstract lists of traits—apply equally to the Music Genome Project? Uniquely as a cultural form, music is non-representational (it cannot easily act as a symbol for an object) and its fundamental physical features (including pitch, rhythm, and timbre) can all be described and modeled using relatively straightforward mathematics. Perhaps this encourages the idea that, like genetic codes, the rich and complex range of music we know and love could be built out of fundamental but relatively simple building blocks. The question is whether our psychological and interpretive responses to music can be mapped as clearly as its physics.

There may be weak and a strong version of the theory underlying the concept of music genomes. The weak version is pragmatic and makes no assumptions about the fundamental structure of music or musical experience. It treats the genes of music, like those listed above, as a form of expert tag. Rather than the informal tags that fans generate in a folksonomy, these tags are like the classifications devised and used by professional librarians in specialist fields. This is all that is needed to power a service like Pandora. A computer can look up the cluster of tags for artists or genres you like, and then recommend other tracks with similar tags.

A strong version of music genome theory could go a lot further than that. It might propose that the genres of music are like different species and that there are fixed and unchangeable differences in their characteristics. Taking a psychological turn, the theory might argue that certain people are naturally more predisposed to particular sorts of music, while other people are drawn to different kinds. If we could just get an accurate psycho-musicological profile of you, we could match you up with the kind of music that resonates with your inner being, as well as screening all new releases for you to filter out those that your profile suggests you will not like.

I have to say that I do not know of any serious advocates of this strong version. As we will see later in this chapter, those who devised the Music Genome Project take a pragmatic approach, recognizing that they do not (at least currently) cover all the aspects of music that people find important. They have adapted their system so that it also takes account of listener feedback about specific tracks when making its recommendations.

The Global Music Relationship Engine, developed by California-based MusicIP (www.musicip.com), represents a slightly different approach, though it too makes only "weak" assumptions about the nature of individual music preferences. MusicIP also has proprietary scales and codes for mapping music and the relationships between different pieces. But, unlike the Music Genome Project or cantometrics, its analysis is done not by trained experts but by computer. If you look closely at a vinyl record, you can see where the loud parts are, and sometimes you can see the actual rhythms of the music in the way the surface of the vinyl reflects the light. In a much more complex and sophisticated way, that is what the computers behind the Global Music Relationship Engine do when they scan a digital music file, and from this they can determine the mood, tempo, and dynamics of the track.

Two big advantages of such automated analysis are scale and speed, which come into play with the enormous volumes of music in the Long Tail. Alan Lomax and his assistant covered 700 recordings in their Global Jukebox. Tim Westergren, the founder of the Music Genome Project, speaks of creating a "musicians' middle class" by facilitating Pandora users' discovery of music beyond the mainstream hits.[62] He envisages a more even distribution of musicians' income, with less extreme differences between those who make it as superstars and those who have to rely on a day job to get by. Yet the Music Genome Project's catalog of over half a million tracks represents only a small proportion of the musicians in the Long Tail. It adds to this at a rate of over 15,000 tracks a month (each track involves 20 to 30 minutes of professional listening and analysis). Many more than 15,000 tracks are released each month, so unless the rate of analysis increases the Project is continually falling behind the total catalog. Its staff listen to everything they receive, but do not add it all to the Music Genome.[63]

By comparison, MusicIP has more than 20 million tracks in its database. With powerful grid computing, it can analyze new tracks in a fraction of the time it would take to listen to them, and with minimal human intervention. This means that the Global Music Relationship Engine can keep on top of an ever-growing universe of music, and could potentially cover everything in the Long Tail.

Similar to Last.fm and Pandora, the Relationship Engine will generate recommendations or a playlist, based on one or more "starter" tracks that you provide as an input. One of the main applications MusicIP advertises is the ability automatically to build playlists based on mood or purpose (such as exercising or driving). For example, a film maker might seek music that conveys a somber mood to underpin a specific scene, while a hotelier wants a different mood to convey the welcoming and relaxed values of his brand. A gym trainer might want music with a particular tempo or "achievement-oriented" dynamics, and a club DJ may want to up the ante gradually as the summer sun goes down.

If you could combine the analyses of the Music Genome Project and the Global Music Relationship Engine, could you build toward a strong theory that predicted what kind of music each individual would like to hear when jogging, or relaxing in the bath? How useful would this be as a means of discovering new music? Imagine the analogy of matching you to dating partners you might like. To help identify potential future partners you submit details of people you enjoyed dating in the past. We have determined (through our genome project) that you like people who are reasonably tall, with dark hair in fairly tight curls, and lower-than-average blood pressure. Furthermore, our relationship engine will be looking out for energetic, bright, "morning" people, who sometimes have quick flashes of temper but soon regain an even keel.

Well, it's a start. If you felt these analyses were accurate, you might be comfortable being provided with a "playlist" of potential partners for you to try out. But I hope you would agree that this is not the whole story; it's just the beginning. I mentioned earlier the criticism that lists of traits do not capture some important features of music, and similarly, in the dating context people know that a chemistry occurs between potential partners that cannot be predicted on the basis of personal characteristics. Let me stress that I do not mean to push this analogy too far by suggesting that pieces of music have a personality you can bond with in the same way you might with another person. However, the appeal of music does depend to some degree on its relationship with its context and its audience. As a simple example, think of a piece of music you already knew, but which suddenly became enhanced for you when you heard it as part of a film soundtrack, at a friend's party, or blowing across the summer air when you were in a boat on a river.

Thus Ian Cross, director of the Centre for Science and Music at Cambridge University, writes:

> Music appears to be a strangely malleable and
> flexible phenomenon. The meaning or
> significance of a musical behaviour or of a piece of
> music can rarely be pinned down unambig-
> uously... Music has a sort of "floating
> intentionality" [the word "intentionality" here
> simply means "aboutness"]; it can be thought of as
> gathering meaning from the contexts within
> which it happens and in turn contributing
> meaning to those contexts.[64]

Perhaps ironically, that connection between music and the
context of listening is one of the things Alan Lomax sought to
describe in his cross-cultural comparisons. Music producer and
composer Brian Eno makes a similar point:

> Music is actually a contingent combination of
> sounds whose emotional resonances are entirely
> dependent on the audience's personal and shared
> histories as listeners. By "contingent" I mean that
> it could have been otherwise. Music didn't have to
> consist of the elements and structures that it
> happens to consist of—and indeed it consists of
> quite other ones in other cultures, as anyone
> attending a concert of classical Thai music will
> soon realise.[65]

So music may be an acoustic phenomenon with a set of
compositional and performance characteristics. But these
acoustic, compositional, and performance factors alone are not
enough fully to explain or predict its appeal. As a means of
shortlisting or playlisting music for discovery these factors may be
useful (just as some physical and social criteria are useful for
shortlisting potential partners on a dating service). But there has

to be some interaction between music and listener—in the form of trying out and auditioning—to build a relationship. You have to be sensitive to the varying characteristics of the listener (including things like mood and alertness) and the context of listening to understand the interaction. Extending the dating analogy, even well-matched lovers sometimes have bad-tempered exchanges. This requirement for sensitivity to context makes it much harder for technology to be able accurately to predict all the tracks that you will like. So I'm afraid you can't give up foraging and working for new discoveries, after all.

The genetics of classical music and video

...**If it's possible** to make recommendations based on analysis of popular music, could a similar approach be applied to other art forms? The Music Genome Project does not yet include any classical music. Its team is working on developing a classical offering, but it remains to be seen to what extent its approach will follow in the footsteps of the academies across the western world that have spent centuries working in closely related fields. Many in the classical music audience, too, have adopted the analysis developed in the academies, and so a genome-based approach may encounter resistance and find it difficult to get a foothold; even though services like Pandora don't require you to follow their analysis, only to appreciate their results.

On the other hand, because it is based on automated analysis of the acoustic and dynamic qualities of audio, you could feed anything into the Global Music Relationship Engine, from John Cage's "silent" 4'33" piece through any other classical work to a recording of the roadworks outside your window. The Relationship Engine would still be able to find tracks with similar mood, ambience, tempo, and dynamics. But it is not clear that it could differentiate between different schools, traditions, and periods of composition, if they shared acoustic and structural features. In some contexts that could be an advantage; it could help classical music listeners break out of hide-bound prejudices and pigeonholes, opening their ears to connections and similarities they had not previously considered.

Video material differs from music in two simple but important ways that affect how easy it is to analyze it and identify similarities between samples. First, video (usually) represents *things*: things like people, buildings and furniture, landscapes, cars, and guns. While well-sighted people find it easy to recognize what moving images represent, it turns out to be very difficult to get computers to do this. Secondly, video (usually) tells a story of some kind. The analysis of narrative is also harder to formalize than, say, the structure of a piece of music with a recurring melody or other motif that has an acoustic "fingerprint." There have, however, been attempts to demonstrate a framework for analyzing narrative. In 1928, structuralist critic Vladimir Propp analyzed the basic plot components of Russian folk tales and generated a framework of their simplest narrative elements. And in 1976 English film writer and director Peter Wollen took this framework and showed how it could be applied to analyzing Hitchcock's film *North by Northwest*.[66] Nevertheless, the idea that such a narrative framework could become a kind of "film genome," used to classify and recommend films, seems faintly ridiculous.

As more computing power and better machine analysis techniques become available, it may be viable to do some automated analysis. Identifying scenes of violence and nudity may be given priority, and the security industries will want to scan video and audio for possible evidence of criminal or terrorist activity. For the time being, however, it is cheaper and quicker to get someone to watch a film and classify it using a standard vocabulary of tags, much as allmovie does currently. Human intelligence still far outstrips artificial intelligence when it comes to analyzing what matters to us in some art forms.

The ambient soundtrack of modern living

...If context is important in understanding our relationship with entertainment and our receptivity to new material, then we need to take into account changes in the accessibility and price of that entertainment as well as accompanying shifts in listening habits. Streams of music and video flow freely from terrestrial, satellite, and cable television, digital and internet radio, as well as many online and hybrid services like those described above as harbingers. CDs and DVDs are given away with magazines as sales promotion tools. Even without taking into account the unlicensed sharing of music and video files, the range of material that you can see and hear, and that feels like it's free, has become enormous.

The film and recording industries are perhaps understandably concerned by the perception this creates that their products have little value. Yet they struggle with the paradox that to market their product, they need to maximize exposure to new material and entice consumers to try it out. There is an argument that people listen less carefully to music that is thrust at them willy-nilly. If you pay $15 or £10 for a compilation of Motown hits, you may want to play it several times to feel you have got value for money. If you receive the same compilation stuck to the front of a magazine, you may just put it on the shelf to be listened to sometime, never. The time when there were scarce opportunities to try out music you might like has passed. Most of us are glad about that and see it as progress.

But with so much readily available entertainment, there's a risk that we become less discerning when we are listening to it and trying it out. Are we seeing "diseases of affluence" when it comes to attentive listening?

That is more or less the conclusion of psychologists at the University of Leicester, following their study of the music listening habits of 346 students, school pupils, workers, and unemployed adults (aged between 13 and 78) as they went about their everyday life.[67] When asked to assess the attention they were paying to the music on a scale from 1 to 10, the participants gave an average rating of 4.8. In their interpretation of the findings, the researchers suggest that "the degree of accessibility and choice has arguably led to a rather passive attitude towards music heard in everyday life." Depending on factors like the time of day, the activities the participants were engaged in (such as driving or relaxing at home), and the company they were in, their choice to listen to music could sometimes be no more than a decision to subject themselves to a form of "sonic wallpaper" as a backdrop to something else. The researchers ask:

> Why do people state that they are so likely to hear music for mundane reasons such as habit and passing the time, rather than in an attempt to achieve the more profound and rewarding experiences that music can undoubtedly produce?

Increasingly we use portable music players for utilitarian purposes, such as managing our mood when commuting. And Apple has partnered with Nike so that its iPods can sense the pace of your footsteps when jogging or working out and adjust the tempo of the music accordingly,[68] turning music into a motivational aid rather than creative expression. Could the same background wallpaper effect apply to video material? The nature of video is that if you're watching it at all, it is harder to let it wash over you or to blank it out. Nevertheless, some people leave their television on all the time, as a companion that is attended to for periods or short glances and then used as background noise.

This is not the first time people have raised concerns about creative communication being diluted by mass media. When radio became widespread in the 1930s, some worried that it was only good at attracting half-hearted attention. The Frankfurt School of social criticism argued that the mass production of cultural objects removed the "aura" of original experiences and cheapened them,[69] and many others have worried about the pervasiveness of Muzak, or the use of music to make for happy shoppers and happy workers.

From our perspective today these concerns seem overstated. Our experience of music is not inferior to that of previous generations—is it? Should we be concerned by this latest research? I don't think so, because the results seem to be consistent with what we would expect as the opportunities people have to try out music become ever more plentiful. Going back to the foraging metaphor, if what you want is scarce, then you will pay close attention to anything that even vaguely resembles it because it only comes along once in a while. But when the kind of stuff you want is readily available, you can afford to become more fussy and discriminating in what you attend to most carefully. If you're listening to the radio or a personalized stream of music from Pandora, you may process most of what you hear in the background, just keeping half an ear out for tracks that particularly appeal and deserve closer attention. If you're listening to a digital music player, there is no need to listen always "in the moment," because you know that you can retrieve any one of the hundreds or thousands of tracks and restart it whenever it suits you.

In *The Recording Angel*, Evan Eisenberg writes:

> While [baroque composer] Albinoni and [jazz trumpeter] Donald Byrd seem to find fulfilment as [sonic] wallpaper... Beethoven seems unhappy in that role. Yet he gets used that way all the time. How lamentable is this? Does everyday life inevitably cheapen art? Isn't art tougher than that—can't it, instead, enrich everyday life, even

> when perceived only glancingly (as, in fact, most
> people perceive architecture)? And where did we
> get the idea that art never gains from rubbing
> shoulders with life?

In the 1970s, Brian Eno felt that some of the novelty of records
and radio had begun to wear off and that listeners did not always
want what the music industry thought they wanted: a lot of
action, variety, and strong voices in their listening to
accommodate their short attention spans.

> To the contrary, I was noticing that my friends and
> I were making and exchanging long cassettes of
> music chosen for its stillness, homogeneity, lack of
> surprises, and, most of all, lack of variety. We
> wanted to use music in a different way—as part of
> the ambience of our lives—and we wanted it to be
> continuous, a surrounding.[70]

In the sleeve notes for his 1975 album *Discreet Music*, Eno wrote:

> I was trying to make a piece that could be listened
> to and yet could be ignored… perhaps in the spirit
> of [French composer of the early twentieth
> century] Satie who wanted to make music that
> could "mingle with the sound of the knives and
> forks at dinner".

One interpretation of the research by the Leicester psychologists
would be that much music listening is tending toward the state that
ambient music encourages. You may give music your close attention
when you hear something you particularly like or when nothing else
is competing for that attention, but for the rest of the time you let
the music work on you just above the threshold of your awareness.

But is this ambient listening necessarily "passive"? Passivity does not seem to be the right characterization of what Eno and his friends were doing, as they were deliberately choosing and sequencing music to meet their needs; they were actively configuring their listening. To what degree can we say that today's listeners to Pandora and Last.fm are emulating them?

Programming your entertainment

...In the new era heralded by the harbingers discussed here, listening (that is, digesting the meaning and value in a piece of music) starts before the needle hits the virtual groove and continues after the tone arm has returned to its virtual rest. The new generation of free-range foragers are programming a wider, more complex range of listening experiences than simply turning on the radio or putting on a CD. The new services create the possibility for different approaches to listening:

- ...Browsing, auditioning, and trying out—the most literal equivalent of foraging for new material—using the free music available through MySpace, Last.fm, subscription and ad-supported services, and all kinds of radio.
- ...Organizing and sequencing music—working out what tracks work well together, and breaking out of the straitjacket of the album.
- ...Playback selection—choosing on the fly from a very large number of albums, playlists, or individual tracks to suit current moods or desires.

The "active" elements of filtering, tagging, managing, and selecting music may account for only a small proportion of your listening. The remainder may appear passive, especially as we increasingly play music while doing something else that may distract us. Nowadays we give more attention to choosing and programming our music than we could in the era of limited choice. A similar pattern applies to watching movies. Now that viewers are freed from the minimal choice of what happens to be on at the local cinema, or on television, they are likely to spend much more preparation, research, and discussion time before they sit down and watch the opening credits roll.

All these actions are active steps in working out how a piece of music or a movie relates to your life and your experience. When you identify that a particular track would work well on your daily commute, to block out the third-rate dance music at the gym, as a soundtrack to a seaside sequence in a home movie, or for your DJ set at a friend's party, you are thinking about music in a way that, a generation ago, was largely restricted to music professionals and a handful of the most dedicated music fans.

As Mark Coleman puts it in *Playback*,[71] his sweeping history of recorded music through the twentieth century, home taping was the first technology to give listeners the "power to program" their own listening experience by creating mix tapes, and personal stereos allowed them to take their programming with them as they went about their lives. The arrival of domestic videocassettes brought a similar level of control to the experience of watching television, albeit without the portability.

The power to program becomes more important as the range of material available to us on demand keeps on growing. It used to be that you would just turn on your television or radio and let someone else do the programming for you. But why be satisfied with that, when you can have something more tailored to your individual interests?

As our personal collections of audio and video grow larger, some of us need help and prompts to remember what we have in our collection and to choose what might fit a particular mood or need; in other words, to rediscover what we've already got. Recommendations and the programming of playlists, then, are not just for discovery, but for adapting and personalizing what we hear (or see) to suit our circumstances.

In his book *Sounding Out the City: Personal Stereos and the Management of Everyday Life*,[72] Michael Bull outlines how different people's listening affects the way they experience urban life. He develops a classification of the different purposes for which we use our personal stereos:

> ...to block out urban sound, controlling our aural environment;
>
> ...to provide a source of absorption (like a book or newspaper), used to mark boundaries in crammed social spaces;
>
> ...to create a personalized, intimate musical accompaniment whenever alone in public;
>
> ...to promote an aesthetic or cinematic experience where what you see is like a film and what you hear is its soundtrack (personalized choice of music is especially important for this);
>
> ...to fill "dead time" (in waiting rooms or busy commuter trains) with personal memories and narratives;
>
> ...to provide a sense of companionship and ward off loneliness;
>
> ...to clear a psychological space, block unwanted thoughts, and manage moods;
>
> ...to make public space more habitable and ward off disturbances (especially for women);
>
> ...to reclaim or repossess time in the face of oppressive routine (performing mindless tasks or a regular commute);
>
> ...to promote a sense of purpose and raise energy levels;
>
> ...to share an exclusive experience with a friend, by taking

one earphone each and joining together in separation
from the rest of the world.

Michael Bull's research provides a social and psychological
context for how we relate to music when listening on the move,
as opposed to, say, listening alone at home or socially in a bar.
Working with iPod users, Bull noticed the pleasure they gain from
being able to switch between different tracks, albums, and
playlists at the drop of a hat. He argues that this enables listeners
to control their space, their time, and their interaction in ways
that enhance the scope to use music for the purposes given above,
such as managing their moods or creating cinematic narratives for
their experiences.[73]

Little comparable research is available on the details of
watching video or playing games while on the move. Intuitively it
seems likely that we use these media for purposes that overlap,
but do not entirely coincide, with what we use music for. Video
and games can fill dead time and provide a source of absorption
as well as, or better than, music. The aesthetic experience is
significantly different, however. Bull describes how the
"soundtrack" of music creates a unique and personal experience
to accompany what people see and feel as they walk city streets.
Video and games tend to occupy both sight and hearing, rather
than providing an accompaniment to other senses. There are also
obvious safety considerations that discourage people from
watching video while crossing the street!

To summarize, Chapter 5 was about the balance between
professional and amateur skills in reviewing entertainment, and
this chapter has focused more on the balance between human and
computer competences. If expert analysis can be encoded in, or
automated by, computers, then this provides a basis for sifting
large volumes of music tracks or text (but not yet video material)
to provide a tailored, personalized experience to listeners. But
after this sifting, much still depends on how you interact with the

music: what you're doing when you hear it, how it's presented (whether accompanied by a video or played in a club, for example), and factors such as what mood you're in. The development of the listener–music relationship is changing as we have more ready access to music, as we use it in more parts of our lives, and as we have increasing power to program it.

Part IV
Technology and technique

7

The new seekers

From the desk at home where I write this, my broadband connection to the net extends my scope for discovering new culture in ways I could only have dreamed of a decade and a half ago. Following any of the TLC strands allows me to explore leads that look interesting. I can try out music on Napster or iTunes and movie clips on Yahoo!; I can consult Wikipedia, allmusic, or the Internet Movie Database to trace the links that radiate from my favourite musicians or actors; and I can keep up with what my friends are listening to and recommending on Last.fm. I am subscribed to three email discussion lists for fans of particular bands, and several more one-way email lists that send me updates about new releases or tours by other bands. Last.fm also updates my diary directly with any nearby concerts by bands that it knows I listen to. Digital music stores send me weekly emails detailing their new releases; three cinemas send me their programs for the week; and I also get regular updates from live music venues, promoters, and a couple of my favorite art galleries. Feeds from the websites I've selected keep me updated on the blogs of celebrities, critics, colleagues, and friends, using their eyes and ears as my filters to pick up on things that they consider worth recording and passing on.

These are all ways in which technology extends the reach of my exploration and foraging. It does this both directly and indirectly through other people. Having seen how discovery works, this part of the book looks in more detail at the ways in which we can make it work better. These include:

...helping consumers forage better (in this chapter);

...helping creators increase their chances of being discovered (in Chapter 8);

...accelerating and amplifying the trends identified in earlier parts, including the growth of the fan economy and the mashing up of professional expertise with amateur enthusiasm (in Chapter 9).

To help us map these possibilities, Marcia Bates, UCLA Professor of Information Studies, has a simple but useful way of classifying different forms of information seeking, which nicely captures both intentional and incidental forms of discovery.[74]

	Active	**Passive**
Directed	Searching	Monitoring
Undirected	Browsing	Being aware

Figure 4 *Modes of information seeking*

From Marcia J. Bates (2002) "Toward an integrated model of information seeking and searching," keynote paper for Fourth International Conference on Information Needs, Seeking and Use in Different Contexts, Lisbon.

In Figure 4, the "directed" modes of seeking are those where you know what you are looking for, whereas "undirected" means you are looking more randomly. "Active" seeking means you are doing something proactively to acquire information (that is, you pull it toward you), while "passive" implies simply being available to absorb information that comes your way without actually seeking it out (it is pushed at you). The active modes of searching and browsing are fairly self-explanatory, particularly with respect to online behavior. If I subscribe to email updates from particular sources, that's an example of monitoring: specifying the kind of information I'm looking for, and then waiting passively to receive further information. On the other hand, if I'm just checking my friend's blog or MySpace profile and she has set it up so that her favorite song of the moment starts playing when I load the page, that's a case of what Bates calls "being aware," being open to the possibility of stumbling across something worthwhile. Techniques for stimulating buzz aim to maximize the chances of us becoming aware of an artist or a product, and will be covered in the next chapter. This chapter deals with how technology can help us search more smartly, browse more effectively, and monitor more widely—without suffering from information overload.

Next-generation search

...**Search engines are** a critical part of life on the net. With practice, most web users are getting increasingly savvy at devising search terms that will get them to the kind of web pages they want. Searching for artists, albums, films, or games is fairly straightforward if you know the title and any other relatively unique names, tags, or data associated with it. But to get to the point where you have both the information and the motivation necessary to do an effective search, you must already have picked up a strong scent that tells you a particular title is going to be up your street. In other words, at least half the journey of discovery is already behind you. But how can searching help you navigate that first half, when you have only a vague idea of the kind of thing you're looking for?

To state the obvious, music and film fans don't know what they don't know, and it's difficult to articulate a search query for something you don't know anything about. Pandora, the interactive "radio" service powered by the Music Genome Project covered in the last chapter, does not expect you to search for the sorts of characteristics identified in the Project, such as "a highly synthetic sonority" or "minor key tonality" (though a handful of these elements, like "an electric guitar solo," might be relevant to some users). Instead, Pandora asks you to search by example. You enter a song title or artist name, and it finds something similar from its database. Often the first results are indeed very similar, and often by the artist you've specified. It's well known that if users don't get good search results on their first try, they quickly give up. So Pandora has to be fairly conservative with its initial suggestions to guard against that. But of course, that conservatism reduces the chances of users making genuinely new discoveries.

As we've seen in earlier chapters, tagging and folksonomies arose partly as an alternative solution to this problem. The idea is that you search using tag terms and that, if others have used the same tags previously, you will be able to find the kind of thing you are looking for. Where large numbers of users and tags are involved, this approach seems to work reasonably well. However, its effectiveness depends on people using the same terms to tag music and films *after* they've tried them out as they might have searched on *before*.

Many search engines are developing their services so that they can better support discovery when searchers are not quite sure what they are looking for. Recognizing that the uncertain explorer may not be able to see the forest for the trees and may be put off by lists of detailed search results, some search engines are giving prominence to results from Wikipedia or allmusic, and even including the first few lines from those overview articles on the search results page.

Another helpful step is for the search engines to model and represent some of the connections and associations between results, or to offer suggestions for related searches. For example, when you search for "All About Eve" it would be helpful to have the results grouped to show those that relate to *All About Eve*, the 1950 Bette Davis film, and those that relate to All About Eve, the British band formed in the 1980s. When you search Ask.com for "Phil Collins," it offers you suggestions for narrowing your search (for example, to Phil Collins tour dates or Phil Collins lyrics), for broadening your search (to Genesis), or for related names (Elton John, Sting, Eric Clapton, Peter Gabriel).

Another way of looking at these suggestions is as the search engine equivalent of the links strand in TLC or as another kind of automated recommendation: "People who searched for Phil Collins also searched for Sting..." In the context of foraging, this is the online counterpart of animals following each other's trails as a means of finding food. In his book *The Search*, John Battelle makes almost exactly this point when he speculates about how people's search explorations—known as "clickstreams"—could be shared:

> What may well become possible in the world of perfect search is the ability to take the clickstream of that journey and turn it into an object—a narrative thread of sorts, something I can hold and keep and refer to, a prop to aid in the telling and retelling of how I came to my answer. Tracks in the dust, so to speak, that others can follow, or question to discover how I came to my conclusions.[75]

Search engines can help in exploration and discovery by analyzing users' clickstreams and then being able to make recommendations based on vague and perhaps confused search queries: "Other people who started looking where you're looking ended up looking over here [possibly in a quite different and apparently unconnected place]."

Finally, search engines will increasingly seek to add multimedia capabilities to their search results so that you can try out the audio and video you are looking for. This will mean that when you search for "All About Eve," you will be able to view a clip from the film or hear a sample by the band; when you search for "Phil Collins," you will be able to hear Sting and Peter Gabriel as well, and judge quickly whether these are avenues you want to explore further. In this way, search engines will improve both the links and the opportunities they provide for trying things out—adding more of the TLC strands—and will better support discovery as a result.

Keeping your eyes peeled

...At the beginning of this chapter I described the mailing lists to which I subscribe and the news feeds that I scan regularly. Some of these are "permission marketing"—agreeing to let niche promoters advertise their services and events to me directly. But all are part of my overall monitoring of what's new and what might be interesting to me. It's a personalized mix that combines both pull and push. "Pull" refers to on-demand access to media, which puts consumers in control over what they get and when. "Push" generally refers to instances where producers control a media channel—typically in television or radio broadcasts—and determine what consumers get. I select the streams and give them permission to push information out to me, which I then pan and sift to see if there is anything there that I want to explore more fully.

Since I have a professional interest in these issues, I cannot pretend that my arrangements and habits are typical. For many people the idea of keeping up with a mass of emails and news feeds is intimidating, even if there's a reasonable chance that some of them may contain interesting information. The usability and targeting of these techniques is not yet sufficiently refined to make their use widespread beyond Savants and Enthusiasts who are willing to invest the time in regular monitoring.

There are two kinds of solution to this problem: a technical kind and a human kind. The technical one involves refining the personalization of permission-based marketing, so that instead of getting emails from each nearby cinema telling you everything it is showing next week, you get just a short message or a notification in your digital diary that sifts and integrates this information, and provides an alert if there any films you might *like* at any of the cinemas. Such services already exist for music: SonicLiving (www.sonicliving.com) styles itself as a "digital to analogue lifestyle converter," and recommends gigs in your city based on what's in your digital music collection. Other fields are further behind because it's not yet so easy to collect data on, say, film collections and preferences.

In the meantime, the alternative to getting technology to sift data is to get other people to sift it for you. When it comes to Galaxie 500 and all things related to them (see Chapter 3), I am only a casual fan compared with the core members of the community that Andy Aldridge started. I don't monitor any developments in that area, other than scanning the community messages. I don't have to, because I can rely on Andy and the others to do it for me. If anything important or interesting crops up, I count on them to flag it. In other domains, blogs fulfill a similar function. Someone who knows and tracks the area more closely than I ever will filters and synthesizes what is going on and draws attention to what seems most important.

The human monitors that work on my behalf may not be quite as compliant as the most usable technology is—they have minds of their own, after all—but by building understanding and rapport with these other like-minded souls, I can keep abreast of a much broader range of sources than would otherwise be possible. They help broaden the horizon of my foraging, with only modest, and often enjoyable, extra effort from me.

Just browsing

...If you're interested in Jack Nicholson, how do you find out that as well as acting in many films, he also directed three and co-wrote a handful of others? If you're interested in the guitarist John McLaughlin, how do you trace his career and his associations with other musicians, from playing as a sideman in Miles Davis's band and other jazz-fusion groups, to being a leading member of the Mahavishnu Orchestra, and releasing several albums as a solo artist and in duets and trios?

Reference sites—Wikipedia, Internet Movie Database, or the All Media Guides—provide one straightforward way of making these links, but they are by no means the only method of exploring connections and enlarging your horizons. By just browsing around, following your nose and your instincts, you pick up a lot of information and start to notice patterns of association. The next generation of web technologies are going to make it easier to trace these associations and easier to store and manage the nuggets you spot as you wander the web.

One of the fundamental steps toward achieving this is to improve the data infrastructure of online information so that it is richer and more standardized. Arguably, the scope to gather information and trace associations from digital music or video files is less than with a CD or DVD, partly because digital files don't have covers. While largely adequate for mainstream pop and rock music, the "cover data" available in Apple's iTunes and Microsoft's Windows Media Player software do not yet provide sufficient means to record the larger ensembles of creators in jazz (band leaders, sidemen, arrangers) or especially classical music (conductors, featured soloists, orchestras).[76] They would be hopeless at accommodating the five-minute scrolling lists of credits that run at the end of some films.

The information you might find on the cover of a CD or DVD is known in technical circles as metadata; literally, data about data. There are differences of opinion about how best to improve it. One camp wants to organize and standardize all the possible metadata you could record about digital files, from band leaders to who owns the publishing rights. They would then seek to encourage all systems to adopt these standards, to maximize interoperability (the ability to take files from, say, the iTunes Store and eMusic, and have their metadata display consistently whatever software you use). The other camp is skeptical about the prospects for achieving agreement on standards beyond those that are already in use,[77] given a competitive commercial environment. They are more inclined to put their faith in bottom-up tagging using folksonomies, combined with powerful search and other technologies for extracting maximum value from these tags. At least in the short term it is likely that both camps will continue to develop their own solutions, with the possibility of some hybrid combination of them further down the line.

Internet commentator (and former philosophy teacher) David Weinberger tends strongly to the bottom-up folksonomy camp. His position is based on an appreciation that you can't just tidy up the data and expect everyone to see it clearly for what it is, so that their browsing will then magically become more rational and efficient. The real world—and the web world—is not like that. A degree of mess and noise will be with us always, and often the "mess" contains subtle cues. As Weinberger puts it:

> We don't process information in the way philo-sophers or computer programmers expect us to. We don't use a systematic set of steps for evaluating what should be believed. Instead we do on the Web what we do in the real world: we listen to the context, allow ourselves to be guided by details we think embody the whole, and decide how much of what this person says we're going to believe.[78]

His observation points to another fact about the way we browse—something that the writers and designers of web resources may not anticipate—that we do not always believe what we read. If we spot cues that undermine the credibility of information, like a wiki page that is littered with typographical errors and has only been edited by one person, we may justifiably doubt what it tells us.

More subtly, we sometimes read *against the grain* of the message that someone is trying to communicate. When a reviewer lauds the new album by an established artist as "a tremendous and welcome return to form," you may infer that the two or three albums that preceded this new release are best avoided. If you have a profile on a social networking site like MySpace, the chances are that, when you look at others' profiles, you are not just checking what they say about themselves but how they say it, and whether they have any extra little features (like a clever animation, say, or a personal video message) that you might like to add to your profile. If they do, you may try to find out how they've created this feature. This is what knowledge-management experts John Seely Brown and Paul Duguid refer to as "stolen knowledge" in their book *The Social Life of Information*[79]: the tendency of free-range foragers to take what they want, rather than what an information provider intends to offer.

As we browse our way selfishly round the web alert for something that might take our fancy, we come up against the problem of keeping track of all the good stuff we find. If we stumble on a patch of information that looks like it might be useful again in the future, we want to be able to find our way back to it. If we come across something that we can harvest straight away, we want to be able to grab it and store it.

For the first of these requirements, more people are using "social bookmarking" services (like del.icio.us and Furl[80]), which enable them to store the location of any web pages they like, add tags to them, and share them with other users. It's the sharing that supports more effective foraging. Like a seagull that spots a flock gathering round a spot on the shoreline, if you see that a web resource has been bookmarked by many other users and is tagged with terms that reflect your interests, that is a good indicator that the resource is worth checking out.

Equally, as more opportunities for trying things out become available on the web, it's useful to be able to store, manage, and review them as easily as possible—like a squirrel or other scavenger putting things aside to come back to later.

New browser software adds multimedia capability to standard web browsers to facilitate your management of audio and video files. MP3tunes (www.mp3tunes.com), for example, offers a plug-in to the popular Firefox browser software so that wherever an audio file appears on a web page, there will be a small button next to it. Clicking on that button automatically saves the file to your private locker on the MP3tunes site—you can then access, view, play, and download the contents of your locker wherever you have a connection to the net. The Songbird browser software (www.songbirdnest.com) is specially designed to help you try out and manage the audio and video files on any web page you visit, giving you a transparent and easy way of storing the files on your own hard disk, plus a means of playing both local and online files through the same user interface.

Gradually the division between what is "out there" on the net and what's "in here" on your PC or iPod is becoming more seamless, and thus it's increasingly straightforward to exploit the rich online pickings.

Making it easier to forage the web and store the fruits of your explorations is bound to be a contentious issue in some quarters, since many MP3 blogs post files that they are not licensed to copy or share. Nevertheless, the makers of the technology powering sites like MP3tunes and Songbird defend themselves by pointing to the noninfringing uses of their software, including sharing of homemade music and video, as well as the files that the record and film industries have chosen to share for promotional purposes.

The point that this chapter reinforces is that, for good or ill, in the digital era consumers are not easily herded by the producer and media industries. If anyone's going to be doing any herding or flocking it is the consumers themselves, aided by the new means for sharing and drawing others' attention to what they think is hot at any moment. Many of us may still be pretty lazy when it comes to seeking out something that excites and inspires us, but the new technologies bring a wider range of foraging methods and sources within our reach, requiring only a little more effort than the television remote handset. The new experience of digital discovery may even mimic some of the same sample-and-select characteristics of channel hopping between stations, trying each one out for a short while before watching the ones that look most interesting—or recording them to watch later. Another way of thinking of it would be bookmarking a whole set of files and then "playing the web" in shuffle mode.

If consumers can't be herded and their attention can't easily be bought, then creators need to find more subtle and canny ways of registering on consumers' radar. One strategy is to make it as easy as possible for foragers to find the creators of their own accord through their searching, browsing, and monitoring. The search engine marketing industry may help creators position themselves to maximize such opportunities. But creators don't want to rely on consumers looking in the right place, so they aim to bring in the fourth quadrant in Figure 4— being aware—to help their work find its audience. With the right bait you can attract large flocks of fans to gather of their own accord and to spread the word about anything they find interesting. The next chapter covers techniques for doing this in the *Net, Blogs and Rock 'n' Roll* era.

8

Buzz building...

Push **marketing may** have passed its mass-media heyday, but it is adapting to the world of the net and blogs, seeking to use them as carriers of "viral" and word-of-mouth messages. These are the kind of messages you become aware of even though you aren't particularly looking for them. To illustrate, I'm going to start this chapter with three stories—the chances are that you may have heard at least one of them before (especially if you're in the UK). But that's kind of the point.

Singer-songwriter José González released his first album in his native Sweden in 2003. It sold relatively well and was widely praised, but the Scandinavian market is not a big one. González and his record label were given the opportunity to license one of his songs, "Heartbeats," for use as the soundtrack to a visually spectacular television ad for Sony in the UK. Another of his songs featured on the soundtrack to American television comedy-drama *The O.C.* The album got a UK release in early 2005 and a US release later that year. Interest grew slowly but steadily, particularly thanks to the ad, which was arresting enough to get people talking (it featured tens of thousands of colorful balls bouncing through the streets of San Francisco) and perhaps asking each other, "And the music's great too, do you know who it's by?" "Heartbeats," the song from the ad, reached No. 9 in the UK singles charts, and the album got to No. 7 and went platinum.

Sandi Thom is another singer-songwriter who took an unusual path to getting the attention of what can often seem like an indifferent public. In early 2006, she didn't have a major record label deal, although she had released a single the previous year that received good radio play. The story goes that she was on her way to play a gig when her car broke down. It was then that she hit on the idea, instead of continuing on a traditional tour, of playing gigs from her basement in south London and making them available to a worldwide audience as a live stream via a cheap webcam. The first gig attracted 70 viewers, but by the middle of the second week the number had increased to 70,000.[81]

Before the series of 21 gigs had come to an end, a mainstream newspaper picked up on the story. And sure enough, it wasn't long before the major record labels paid a visit to the basement. Sandi Thom signed her deal live on the webcam, and less than three months later her re-released single became a No. 1 hit. Her album went straight to the top the week after it was released. (As I write, Thom is embarking on a conventional tour of the UK and the west coast of America. We must assume she now has more reliable transport.)

And then there's *Snakes on a Plane*. The film nearly had its title changed, but the story surrounding that and its well-what-do-you-think-it's-about candor is what made it one of the most talked about and anticipated films of 2006. It's often difficult to trace the origins and development of word-of-mouth phenomena, but the buzz surrounding this film seems to date back to a blog post by the screenwriter Josh Friedman, who was offered—but failed to take up—the opportunity to develop the script. Readers were amused and captivated by both his amusing comments on the zen mantra nature of the title, and by the prospect of what actor Samuel L. Jackson might bring to such an apparently hokey concept. So captivated, in fact, that they started creating their own promotional materials for it: posters, songs, mock trailers, competitions, impressions of Robert de Niro and Jack Nicholson auditioning for parts. Intrigued individuals did all of this without knowing much more about the film than its title, and they shared their creations via blogs and social networks.

Again the mainstream media picked up on the buzz and started commenting on it, mainly as a story about blogging and user-generated content. But of course, they couldn't help but give the film more publicity in the process. Having changed the name of the film (to the more anodyne *Pacific Air Flight 121*), the film studio bowed to pressure from the blog community and, allegedly, from Samuel L. Jackson himself, and changed it back. Indeed, it very much decided to ride the wave of fan feedback. It even shot additional scenes to bring the film more in line with the expectations fans had expressed, and in some territories did not allow the mainstream media to see previews of the film before its opening, preferring to trade on the head of steam that had already built organically.

As it happened, while expectations were raised very high for *Snakes on a Plane*, it grossed just over $15 million at the US box office in its opening days. This was half what some analysts had been predicting, but arguably still an impressive figure for a film about, well, snakes on a plane. Perhaps although everyone registered the film's existence and its basic concept, a sizeable number, armed with this accurate understanding, were able to discern that it wasn't really for them.

Blowing in the wind

...These stories share several characteristics. Each shows how an artist or film can break through and capture the attention of a mass audience—an audience that may not be particularly alert to the possibilities of discovering new sources of entertainment. Think, for example, of the Indifferent music listeners we met in Chapter 2. The Project Phoenix research suggested they are unlikely to be searching, browsing, or monitoring developments in the music scene: "They will happily let most content wash over them—their relationship with music is quite passive and 'lean backward' in nature."[82] Perhaps they are watching *The O.C.*, or maybe they are watching football on television when the Sony/José González advertisement comes on. The first time it mostly washes over them, but the visual element is novel enough to make sure they pay slightly closer attention on subsequent viewings. Gradually González's music insinuates its way into their consciousness. Of course, they don't know who the music is by yet. That's where the conversations with friends or work colleagues come in. If they're sufficiently intrigued, this may even be the point where they start foraging more actively for information. In the UK there happens to be a website (www.tvadmusic.co.uk) set up specifically to help people identify and locate the music from television ads.

It's unlikely that many people indifferent to music were among the 70,000 who logged on to Sandi Thom's webcast. You would expect it to be music Savants and Enthusiasts—and industry players from record labels—who picked up the first rumblings of online word of mouth, and it probably was. But the ultimate payoff came not with the 70,000 web users, but with the secondary audience—a handful of record label executives, journalists, and radio producers, plus a mass of casual radio listeners, television watchers, and newspaper readers—who sat up and took notice when they heard the story about the 70,000. In other words, the webcast gigs on their own could not have got Sandi Thom a No. 1 single and album, but the publicity they generated could. In fact, in the wake of Thom's success, controversy was stirred up when skeptical bloggers and journalists started to question whether the webcast story was a scam conceived to get wider attention. We'll come back to that later in the chapter.

In their different ways, José González and Sandi Thom have managed to register on the radar of people who might never have discovered them otherwise. Think of those people as just going about, minding their own business, when they catch the scent of something that might be interesting. Smell is a sense you can't turn off, and scents are borne towards you on the wind so they reach you even when you're not attending to anything (whereas you might miss seeing something if you're looking the wrong way or not paying attention).

A new form of marketing and promotion has grown up that seeks to find a "carrier" for your message or product that will get dispersed over a wide area, so that as many people as possible catch the scent. The carrier and the message need not be directly related, as long as they are yoked together so that the message always gets across.

In José González's case, the carrier is an innovative advertisement that someone else (Sony) has paid for, to ensure it will be widely seen. González wins every way. He receives a "synchronization" fee from Sony for the rights to use his performance, and he gets the kind of repeated exposure that his wistful music probably needs to catch on with a broad public. (Sony also gets to bask in the reflected glory of association with a young artist on the up, so it can feel its money is well spent on enhancing its brand.)

In Sandi Thom's case, the carrier is a human-interestmeets-cyberspace story that comes across like a modern fairytale. A young, pretty woman struggles to make her way in the world with some homespun songs. Faced with adversity (the brokendown car playing the role of fairytale carriage), she turns necessity into the mother of twenty-first-century invention and friends come to the rescue (the webcast streaming was gifted from the company that provided it). Even the basement where the gigs were webcast has an air of Cinderella about it. This leads the suitors (major record labels) to her door, and finally she can go to the ball. Are you intrigued to hear the songs that fuel this story now? Of course you are. Even if, like many a fairytale, it were to turn out to be too good to be true, you're hooked.

As for *Snakes on a Plane*, the initial carrier there seems to be simply the mantra of the title and the Samuel L. Jackson catchphrase ("I've had it with these m*f*king snakes on this m*f*king plane"), but this replicated itself like some mutant gene into other carriers—the joke songs, trailers, and fan fiction, all of which stayed true to the simple message at the core of the film.

There are various names given to the growing craft and different ways of catching attention by causing a stir or piggybacking one thing on another, infectious one: buzz, viral, or word-of-mouth marketing; blog and stealth marketing; and ambient advertising. This is the new generation of "push" techniques. Where past generations of mass advertising and hype sought to direct and herd consumers toward their products, the new generation is more subtle, more inclined to tease and flirt with its audience, hoping to pique their curiosity. (In this respect some buzz methods involve elements of pull as well as push; as we saw in the last chapter, the distinction sometimes becomes less clear outside mass broadcast media.)

The rest of this chapter elaborates on this range of techniques, including how to get your material exposed to a potential audience, how to get people talking about it, and how to get them to pass it on to their friends.

Spreading the seed

...Seeds are blown in the wind. Some fall on paths and tarmac, some fall on stony ground where there is little soil, some fall among other seeds and plants that grow faster and smother any growth—and some fall on good soil where they take root and flourish. Some seeds have evolved in special ways so they are blown further. Other seeds have ingenious burrs so that they stick to passing birds or insects, who then unwittingly carry them far and wide.

You could think of the diverse ways in which entertainment gets spread about in similar terms. It used to be that pluggers would seek to get records played on the radio, film studios would release trailers to cinemas and (sometimes) television, and promoters would hope for favorable reviews in the press. In-store displays and PR events were additional means of raising awareness. Radio and television continue to be very important channels for discovery (see Chapter 11). But now they are complemented by podcasts, online "viral" video clips, ringtones, and wallpapers for mobile and desktop screens. Consumers can remix and mash these up to personalize them and include them in blogs or profiles on social networking sites like MySpace and its competitors.

And it's not just individuals who use music and playlists to project their identity, as Sony's licensing of relatively unknown new music for a big-budget advertisement indicates. The brand communications industry is very keen to project its clients by associating them with the right profile of cool music and visuals. In 2006, spirits company Bacardi launched what it claimed was the first brand-funded global radio station, broadcast via the internet and mobile phone networks. Around the same time, Westin Hotels and Resorts contracted digital retailer eMusic to create and develop a signature music playlist for its properties around the world to "help define the global voice of the Westin brand."[83] In this case the playlist forms part of the lobby environment and in-room entertainment, but may also serve as ambient advertising for the tracks and artists included on it.

In the case of music, an important factor in gaining traction with a potential audience is repeat exposure. Often it takes more than one listen for the charms of a song to make themselves known to us. In an era where many nonmainstream artists find it difficult to get included in radio playlists and more radio stations vie for our listening time, radio is gradually becoming a less reliable way of achieving repeat exposure. So the challenge in a fragmented media landscape is to get your seed blown far and wide, so that as people wander that landscape, their chances of coming across it are as high as possible.

There's a wrong way and a right way of going about this. Conducting mass campaigns of "spam" messages via email or comments on blogs that link back to your song may get some short-term results, but won't do your reputation much good.

The right way is to make it easier for others to help spread your seed. As co-author of the book *The Future of Music*,[84] Gerd Leonhard has articulated a manifesto for what he calls "music like water," where access to music "on tap" will become like access to a utility service, with personalized streams available to you at home or on the road over a ubiquitous wireless network. Showing that he is prepared to walk the talk, Gerd is also founder and CEO of Sonific, a start-up that aims to make music available for you to include on your blog, on photo- and video-sharing sites, even in eBay listings, and in any other online content you create. Sonific's SongSpots service (www.sonific.com) is free, provided that your use helps promote the music you choose and is noncommercial (that is, it does not form part of a service from which you stand to make a profit). Visitors to your blog hear the full tracks and can click to get more information or to buy them. So you get free music to enhance your web presence, and the artists get free exposure.

At the time of writing, almost all of the 40,000 artists whose music is available via Sonific are unsigned artists or on independent labels. This reflects a perhaps unsurprising division between, on the one hand, those artists for whom exposure to a wider audience is the primary consideration and, on the other, those with considerable major-label investment behind them, for whom the primary concern is protecting and recouping that investment. Thus it is mostly the music from the former camp that is experimenting and innovating at the edges of the net, while the major players by and large stick to more established or tightly regulated solutions.

One means of light regulation by which the independent sector can facilitate the spread of its music without losing all control is the new range of Creative Commons licenses for sharing copyright material. These are based on copyright law but, instead of "all rights reserved," they proactively permit some uses, thus becoming "some rights reserved." There are different types of license with different permissions, but the most common one for sharing music allows you to copy a track to share it with your friends as much as you like, as long as you identify who made it and no one makes any money from the copying (that is, it is noncommercial).

Magnatune is an independent record label that licenses recordings of all its artists under Creative Commons, so that you can hear them, in full and for free, on its website (www.magnatune.com). In four years it has released music from 200 artists, using blogs, social networks, and word of mouth to help promote the site and its artists. As John Buckman, Magnatune founder, puts it, "the main marketing technique is getting people to listen to our music, whether as full-album previews on the site, or our own [online] radio stations and podcasts, or via other people's podcasts and their web sites."[85]

Imagine that you make podcasts, a form of audio blogging using downloadable files instead of text, and would like to include music in them, either as background or as a feature in your discussion. Magnatune grants you a free license to use any of its music in your podcasts for free, even if this use is "commercial-but-poor" (which is defined as making a gross profit from podcast-related activities of less than $1,000 per year). These podcasts are the equivalent of the insects that carry your seeds far and wide, so it's best to make those seeds as light and sticky as possible.

Of course, not everything can be free, but Magnatune makes even commercial licensing of its music—for ads, films, compilations, and suchlike—as straightforward as possible. No haggling between lawyers—you identify the music you want from the website, and then step through an online "wizard" process that concludes with you being sent a valid legal agreement and a CD-quality version of the music.

Lonelygirl15, a fictional video diary that became one of the first big hits devised specifically for YouTube and MySpace, used music from Magnatune and other sources licensed under Creative Commons. Millions of online viewers got to hear artists that they wouldn't otherwise have heard. As *Lonelygirl15* took off and started to make money, its makers paid for new licenses to cover commercial use of the music, with the payment being shared between Magnatune and its artists.

Will major labels come round to this low-friction attitude to letting their music spread via the net? There have been rumors that some may have tacitly allowed album tracks to find their way on to peer-to-peer services as a way of monitoring which connected best with an audience and to help them choose which to release as singles. Artist videos seem to be another means of testing the water. Videos were initially produced as a means to promote music sales, rather than to generate revenue in themselves. Record labels licensed Yahoo! to provide music videos on demand (while looking covetously at the advertising revenues Yahoo! generated from this service). They then struck a deal with Google that not only enabled it to put videos on its own site, but also licensed other websites using Google's AdSense advertising platform to display videos on their sites, with revenues split between the labels and the website publisher. This may see music video being legally incorporated in a wide range of blogs and other niche websites. Whether this step could ultimately help open the door to the "music like water" scenario—where you would pay a license fee or levy for on-demand access to all the music in the world—remains to be seen.

Spreading the word

   ...What's the advantage of having your material reach the eyes and ears of an audience via a bunch of blogs, many of which may only have a few hundred readers, when you could be using channels that measure their reach in millions (Yahoo!, Rhapsody, or broadcast media)? Of course, these options are not mutually exclusive, and not everyone has the clout to achieve the latter. But the former represent what might be called the Long Tail of promotion; that is, none of the blogs individually may count for much, but collectively the number of people they reach is significant.

   There is another reason that getting bloggers to spread the word matters more than the raw numbers might indicate. It's the word-of-mouth effect. You may see lots of advertisements telling you how reliable Volvo cars are; you may read reviews that quote statistics and suggest this claim is justified; but if someone you meet at a party happens to be one of a tiny minority who had a bad experience with an unreliable Volvo, you can't help giving disproportionate weight to this account. You get a first-person narrative, which seems so much more immediate than glossy ads and dry statistics, and you empathize directly with the person describing their ordeal, even if she was a complete stranger to you only half an hour previously.

   Reading a good blog can be a bit like that. It has the personal touch that lends it an immediacy and authenticity we don't get from more mass-scale professional media. It's unsurprising that some in the marketing industry have started to look into the possibilities of exploiting the extra salience that opinions and recommendations take on when expressed through blogs. Thus Andrew Corcoran and colleagues write:

> Blog marketing puts credibility back into the
> marketing mix: In an era where people are

> increasingly sceptical of traditional interruptive advertising, dismissing overt commercial messages as propAdganda [sic] and corporate spin-wash, blogs represent a refreshing and credible source of information. Readers are more likely to believe information in an opinion-leading third-party blog than in an ad, whilst the informal style of avoiding sales-speak and overt promotion in business blogs enhances the credibility of the medium.[86]

From this quote you can probably see that when it comes to blog marketing, there's also a right and a wrong way to go about it. The cynical, short-term approach would be to reintroduce into blogs a more insidious kind of spin-wash under the cloak and pretense that it comes from independent third parties. In online communities in 2005, there were allegations that a PR campaign had posted identical messages to several internet forums in an attempt to limit the damage of a poorly received television performance by US star Ashlee Simpson.[87] Clearly, if you take advantage of a medium with a reputation for authenticity by repeatedly adding spin-wash to it, you make it less authentic— people become wary of what they read in blogs and everybody loses.

In the era of *Net, Blogs and Rock 'n' Roll*, being in touch with grassroots fans, being authentic, and being seen to be authentic are critical attributes—especially for entertainment that is aimed at an older, more wary audience. Managers and promoters will go to considerable lengths to paint themselves out of the picture, as if their artist's music had such luminescent qualities that it found a large audience through a natural and inevitable process, and all they did was respond to the audience and the process. Thus José González's official website tells us:

> It's uplifting then, in an age of spin, hype and
> wall-to-wall hyperbole, to note that José's music
> has required no lavish production (he records on
> basic equipment, at home), no exotic packaging or
> gimlet-eyed marketing strategies, to make it
> cherished by thousands.[88]

The Sandi Thom story appears to tell a similar tale. However, first bloggers, and then journalists, started to wonder if they smelt a rat in that webcast basement. They doubted the story of how the webcasts had come about and the viewing figures that were claimed. Most damningly, they speculated as to whether the deal with the major record label might have been done *before* the online tour, which might have meant that the whole story was a clever PR stunt. Thom's manager categorically refuted this. He insisted that the fundamentals of the story were true, while conceding that the PR company had been interested in an angle to take to the press, and that the story had been whipped up a bit through the kind of Chinese whispers that inevitably get passed on when there is interest from major media and record labels.[89]

Given that the blog world seems to be policed by such skeptical citizens, what is the right way to get people talking about your material and spreading the word via blogs and online forums? Idil Cakim, director of knowledge development at PR firm Burson-Marsteller, suggests, "Any marketing initiative that is not based in honesty and transparency is bound to fail somewhere along the line."[90] He suggests developing relationships with the group of Originators and Synthesizers who seek information about new material and have developed a trusted position in their online communities (Cakim calls them E-fluentials, but, as I suggested in Chapter 3, the terms are effectively synonymous). You can provide them with updates, material for review, and interesting stories—just as you might with the mainstream media—but it's wise to be transparent about this, and expect these Originators to be at least as independently minded as their mainstream counterparts. You can't anticipate getting nothing but good reviews and positive recommendations in return for favors and freebies. And even if you did, what backlash might there be if and when word of the favors and freebies got out?

Some online ventures are seeking more subtle ways to incentivize bloggers and online advocates. Amazon has operated an affiliate program for some years now, which allows website owners and bloggers to earn a modest commission (up to 10%) on any sales to customers who arrive at Amazon's site via their own site. Amazon now enables you to build your own store (an "aStore"), which features your selections from Amazon's inventory in web pages with your own logo and color branding. So if you have a fan site or blog on Tom Cruise films, you can include on it a store with all the relevant DVDs, soundtrack albums, and books. There is enormous scope for highly specialist stores that Amazon could never develop itself—from American showtunes from the 1920s and 1930s to books about Egyptian history. People who invest time and expertise in building a strong reputation for their blogs and aStores can even find themselves making good money.

Weedshare (www.weedshare.com) has been running a scheme for several years that encourages you to share digital music files with your friends via email, instant messenger, or your website. These friends can listen to each file three times for free, but then have to pay to enable unlimited further plays. If they do, you get a commission. Like Amazon, this affiliate route to purchase is only a supplement to the "front door" retail route of shopping direct at Weedshare's store. But in the case of another digital music sales platform, BurnLounge (www.burnlounge.com), customers can only buy via a BurnLounge member. The concept is to turn fans into retailers. BurnLounge gives enthusiasts the platform and tools to become part of the entertainment business.

There are three levels of operating your own online store, effectively as a hobby, as a part-time revenue generator, or as a real business. The reaction to BurnLounge on some digital music blogs has been very circumspect,[91] implying that the model was a multilevel marketing scheme, and that it would be very difficult for fans to recover the costs of subscribing without selling large amounts of music.

Blog culture draws a line between what is an acceptably modest level of commercialism and what is so commercial as to cloud the authenticity of communication. Magnatune's definition of "commercial-but-poor" captures the spirit here. It's one thing to be generating enough revenue to cover costs; it's another to be making a living off the proceeds. Commenting on the move to allow MySpace members to sell music via the MySpace site, music industry manager Terry McBride said, "We have a strong belief the next major retailer in music is the consumer themselves."[92] The indications are that for this to happen, consumers must remain fans first and foremost, and retailers a distant second.

Successful engagement with blog culture requires promoters to meet it on its own terms of transparency and independence. If you do this, you will earn the reputation and trust that form the principal currency of bloggers. Blog culture embraces the idea of doing favors, but hates the taking of bribes. Of course, trust and reputation don't guarantee you good reviews and recommendations—as ever, some seeds fall on stony ground and some fall on good ground.

Propagating the virus

...It's one thing to get people talking about a new film or music track, but it's another to create a conversation that spreads itself. That's like your seeds not just germinating, but also maturing quickly and producing their own seeds. When bloggers pick up on someone else's blog post and blog about it themselves, and that leads to yet more people spreading the word via their blogs or emails, that's when you create a real buzz.

The ease, speed, and global reach of digital platforms mean that buzz can grow faster and penetrate further than ever before. Moreover, word of mouth on these platforms leaves a trace that is measurable to some degree.[93] Consequently, marketers are exploring ever more seriously how to spread digital text, audio, and video through social networks to raise awareness for their clients. As buzz marketing expert Paul Marsden writes in *Connected Marketing*:

> Of course, many products are not exciting enough, on their own, to get talked about. What viral, buzz and word of mouth campaigns do is add the excitement necessary to get them talked about. When this happens, opinions get shared and superior products benefit, but bad products suffer: viral, buzz and word of mouth campaigns don't create word of mouth in a vacuum: they unlock, stimulate and accelerate the natural word of mouth potential of your product.[94]

Not every new album, film, or game is any more exciting than just another new album, film, or game. The marketing and promotional expertise then comes into its own, and the challenge is to do "something remarkable" that gets it talked about, or to create an exciting branded message, video, or game that people will forward to their friends. In the case of José González this happened more or less by accident when Sony approached him to use his music in an advertisement that turned out to be quite spectacular. Artists like Nizlopi in the UK and OK Go on both sides of the Atlantic have created infectious (and very cheaply produced) videos that people couldn't help sharing with their friends via email and YouTube. These videos are credited with getting both artists into the charts in an increasingly crowded marketplace. To tie in with their *Year Zero* album, the cult band Nine Inch Nails devised an elaborate scheme that encouraged fans quite literally to forage for clues. The band and its agency created a series of pointers and hoax organizations, spread across tour t-shirts, conspiracy theory websites, and an alternate reality game, which required fans to search the web to piece together a complex and Orwellian narrative, linked to the album's concept about the state of the world in 2022.[95]

As Paul Marsden's quote makes clear, however, stirring up excitement will only work effectively if the product has the "legs" to build on the momentum that the excitement creates.

In recent years the buzz approach has sometimes taken a reflexive twist, where the "something remarkable" that gets talked about is simply that something is being talked about a lot online. Future generations will surely find it unremarkable and taken for granted that the net and grassroots communications have the potential to build mass awareness for new entertainment. But for now, at this turn-of-the-century point in our history, such happenings are often considered newsworthy by the mainstream media. This offers buzz marketers a double win (as we saw in the case of Sandi Thom): reaching a significant audience online *and* having newspapers, magazines, and television amplify this effect by telling their audience about it.

In 1999, the independent film *The Blair Witch Project* set the first template for this effect by creating a story around how successful its unorthodox online marketing campaign was proving to be. Following the spread of online word of mouth about the film's website (which claimed it to be a documentary when it was fiction), the traditional media picked up on the story. At the height of the dot-com boom, the media were especially on the lookout for news of revolutionary online techniques. *Time* magazine made it a cover story. Of course, this raised awareness further and led to more people, who might never have caught the online buzz, finding out about the film and its website. (At the time, on the basis of this runaway success, some excited commentators predicted a wave of highly profitable low-budget films, with dire consequences for big Hollywood productions and marketing methods. However, a year later, against the background of the dot-com crash, the story had changed: *The Blair Witch Project* was declared to be a one-off.[96])

The rise of the UK band Arctic Monkeys in their home country followed a similar storyline at the time leading up to and immediately after their first releases. News of an online "underground" buzz about the band percolated into the mainstream media around the time they released a first limited-edition single. Traces of this early buzz proved difficult to find online, but that, perhaps, is a sign of how underground it was. Hip radio stations played the single, as a badge of how hip they were to be in on the buzz. When the national newspaper *The Guardian* asked a set of influential tastemakers the question "Who's going to be big?", the people who cited the Arctic Monkeys included the editor of the UK's major weekly music magazine, producers of two high-profile music television programs, the country's biggest youth music radio station, the largest music retailer, and Amazon UK.[97] This was two weeks before the band's first full-release single came out. With such mainstream backing, were they still an underground phenomenon by then?[98] The Arctic Monkeys had become poster boys for the net-driven word-of-mouth phenomenon. That a key element of their story was how much other people were discussing them captures the essence of self-fueling viral methods: buzz about buzz creates more buzz.

However, this also points to an inherent limitation in buzz marketing as a means for maximizing discovery. By definition, buzz makes you stand out above the crowd. But if everyone uses the same techniques equally effectively, everyone gets the same lift and no one stands out. Buzz artists and films are like fast-growing vines that choke the growth of other seeds and plants. There can only be a few winners.

Going for the slow burn

...There is an alternative to the buzz-driven approach that is less dependent on headline-grabbing gimmicks for gaining exposure. It's more of a slow-burn method and even harder to target, so it may be harder for marketers to sell to their clients, but for some material it may be more effective in the long run. Instead of being driven by the audience's interest in remarkable content, this approach is driven by their interest in each other and in relationships. Instead of trying out a track because it has a spectacular video or fairytale story attached, you try it out because it's attached to the profile of someone you want to get to know better.

MySpace has been the pioneer in successfully implementing an online system that encourages the propagation of music and video through a network of social relationships, though the growth of the ringtones market preceded it by a few years. You personalize your MySpace profile and your mobile phone so they say something about you. It's part of the way you project your identity in public spaces, hoping that by doing so you will attract others who share your tastes and attitudes.

Critically, this socially driven use of audio and video draws in not just Savants and Enthusiasts, but Casuals and even Indifferents as well. For young people especially, the peer influence is clear. You want to be seen as interesting and individual, don't you? Well, how are you going to do that if you have a factory-standard ringtone or a social networking profile with no audio? And if you're going to have one of these audio accessories, you're going to have to do some auditioning to choose one that projects the right message.

Is this any more than the digital equivalent of drawing the logo of your favorite band on your school bag or playing music to set the ambience of your dorm room? Even if that was all there was to it, this use of music as a marker of individual identity and group affiliations is what drove the market for popular music in the first place. The digital dimension takes it beyond that as well.

A key requirement for harnessing the potential of social networks to gain exposure for your material is to make it as easy as possible, legally and technically, for people to spread it to their contacts. We covered some of the legal and licensing issues earlier in the chapter. Matt Locke has coined the term the "tearable web" to refer to the technical means for using audio, video, and other material in online profiles and blogs. This is the idea that you can treat web pages like those in a magazine or newspaper: tear a bit off and stick it in your personal scrapbook. In the personal multimedia era, the growth in such digital scrapbooks is rapid and enormous, from clippings about your favorite stars to autobiographical blogs to digital photos and holiday videos. Some parts of the digital scrapbook of your life will be just personal mementos, but there are other parts you want to share with your friends and family. You can draw from this resource selectively to describe and present yourself in different settings, including social, professional, and dating networks.

Sonific SongSpots are an example of the tearable web. YouTube enables you to take your own or someone else's video clips and include them in your blog or social networking profile. Flickr's photo-sharing service provides various ways of incorporating your photos in other web pages. Many music services make it easy for you to "tear" parts of your personal music data and stick them elsewhere on the web. The playlist-sharing service FIQL (www.fiql.com) lets you include your playlists wherever you like. With Last.fm, you can tear a list of your most recent tracks, or your most frequently played tracks and artists, and you can change the layout and color scheme of these lists to match the page where you want to put them. You can also share a stream of your personal "radio" stations.

Long after the excitement and viral potential of a particular piece of compelling content has worn off, people will still be interested in each other, in developing new relationships and exploring each other's tastes and collections of music and video. The two approaches—content focused and relationship focused—are not mutually exclusive, of course. In fact, they are most successful when combined and one factor drives or accelerates the other. In the next chapter, we'll see how new online techniques such as the tearable web can support these kinds of synergies and maximize the potential for new discoveries.

9

Accelerating digital discovery...

The vast numbers of songs, books, films, and games in the Long Tail are, by definition, not hits. They appeal to niche audiences and, even with sophisticated communication tools and databases, it can be difficult to get a fix on these people and target promotions at them effectively.

That, along with increasingly on-demand access to media, is partly what leads Chris Anderson, in *The Long Tail*, to place his emphasis on people finding stuff, rather than stuff finding people. But there's more to it than that, as there's a cultural shift in the way markets work when the momentum switches from "push" to "pull." When you're dealing with niches, it's more like herding cats than herding cattle. In an article titled "From push to pull: The next frontier of innovation," the management theorists John Seely Brown and John Hagel write:

> In "push" systems generally, the core assumptions are that companies and other institutions can anticipate demand and that mobilising scarce resources in previously specified ways is the most efficient and reliable way to meet it... [But] the highly specified, centralised and restrictive nature of push systems prevents companies from experimenting, improvising, and learning as quickly as they might, both throughout their own organisations and across others.[99]

They go on to stress the need for flexibility in responding to unpredictable demands. As the Oscar-winning screenwriter William Goldman notoriously said of the Hollywood establishment's ability to predict a hit film, "Nobody knows anything... Not one person in the entire motion picture field knows for a certainty what's going to work. Every time out it's a guess."[100]

The solution to unpredictable demand, Seely Brown and Hagel argue, is systems that are geared to respond to "pull" from the market and from audiences. Such systems are built on a platform of loosely coupled modules rather than tightly integrated programs. They are people centric rather than resource or information centric. And they focus on innovation rather than efficiency, with a willingness to let solutions emerge organically rather than trying to engineer them in advance. It's these modular, organic, pull-oriented platforms that this chapter will discuss, showing how new platforms and software services can help you forage more efficiently and effectively.

It may seem premature and perverse to dismiss top-down, highly integrated models at a time when Apple's iPod, iTunes software, and iTunes Store combined have become, by some distance, the dominant commercial platform for portable digital audio and video. The main plank of its success has been the close integration of hardware, software, and commerce platform to create a seamless user experience. Apple achieves this by hiding the complexities of file formats and rights management. The problems come when you try to move your audio and video on to non-Apple devices—it's often tricky to do so.

It is possible to treat the distribution, transaction, and playback of media files as a closed system. It *isn't* possible to treat discovery and exploration in the same way. Discovery blows on the wind. Crossing boundaries is part of what it's about. You read a review of a re-released print of the film *Imitation of Life* in a magazine, you search for its trailer online, check out which other films the director and lead actors have been involved in to see whether you can remember liking them or not. You may scan a professional review, then look at how other people have tagged the film, and check a five-star and a one-star audience review to see what they liked and didn't like about it. Once you've decided to see the film, you want to find out whether it's showing at a cinema nearby, how you can buy or rent a DVD, whether it's available for download, or if it might be shown on television in the near future. After you've seen and enjoyed it, you may look for more films like it, and continue your exploration in this direction.

It's possible that Google or Amazon, or some combination of the two, may at some point provide a service that enables you to carry out most of the steps above without leaving its web territory ("site" seems too diminutive a word to describe such a broad dominion).[101] But even if it were, such an ambitious landgrab would inspire considerable competition. Remember from Chapter 5 that the architecture of the net is not friendly to anyone trying to establish a gatekeeper role. There are always ways round any gate, which competitors and anyone who wants to challenge the gatekeeper's authority will exploit. Secondly, any company establishing such a dominant position will not own and manage each of the steps above directly. They will act more like a switchboard for getting the information to you than a proprietor of and repository for that information.

In fact, Google and Amazon are examples of businesses that have led the way in recognizing that the way to cater for unpredictable demand is to provide an enabling platform and encourage others to adopt and adapt this platform to meet niche demands that Google or Amazon would find it difficult to anticipate itself. Thus, for example, Google enables third parties to combine their own data with the Google Maps application to provide interactive displays that show the location of events on local maps, such as the cinemas showing *Imitation of Life* that are nearest to you. And Amazon's Marketplace can connect you to sellers who can offer you *Imitation of Life* on a new or second-hand DVD at a bargain price.

Crucially, in these examples the third-party providers remain independent and free of any exclusive deals. If someone else comes up with a better platform to help them meet demand, then they could switch to that platform more or less at the drop of a hat—or, more likely, they could use multiple platforms at once.

Thus the prescription in this chapter concentrates not on automating the discovery process in any way that might seek to centralize and constrain it, but on accelerating the process whereby discovery can ripple through the audience. This spread is powered by the relationships between us in the audience—our desire to share our latest finds—and facilitated by the new generation of net technologies.

In the *Net, Blogs and Rock 'n' Roll* recipe, the net is the platform that enables us to pull what we want on demand, blogs represent the diversity of voices and people-centric routes to discovery, and rock 'n' roll is the organic approach to innovation and the attitude that values exuberance over diligence and desire over control.

The net: Build on the power of the network

...Earlier in the book we saw several cases where the usefulness and effectiveness of services grew as the number of users and the level of activity increased. Tagging of films, books, songs, and suchlike is a straightforward example. If only a few people tag only a few items, these tags are not going to be very useful for getting an overview of the full range of what's available.

A similar effect comes into play with recommendations that are based on collaborative filtering. I might listen to a relatively unknown band (deep in the Long Tail) and, if the music service I'm using has only 100,000 users, it's possible that few if any of the other users will have also listened to that band. So if the service makes any recommendations to me on the basis of "people who like this band also like..." they will be pretty hit and miss. A service with millions of users, however, or one that targets fans of the kind of band I'm listening to, will be more likely to have data from several other followers of the band, so their recommendations will be more robust.

With wikis, if the "1% of users are Originators" rule of thumb applies (see Chapter 3), you need hundreds of users to stimulate effective collaboration and generate valuable material. Then you may need thousands of eyeballs to keep an eye on the material, for example to correct minor errors or be watchful if an unscrupulous advertiser starts inserting promotional messages on wiki pages in an attempt to boost traffic to its own website.

To attract more fans to use these services, there has to be a benefit and a payoff for them. That, after all, is the basis on which the net grew in the first place: by encouraging people and organizations to contribute resources and information at no charge *in their own self-interest*. Fans tag songs and videos not because they fancy doing some volunteer librarianship in their spare time, but because it will help them find and organize these items in the future (by tagging songs with "gym" or "driving," for example, they can make it easier to compile a playlist later to accompany these activities). It may also help them share these items with friends, to express their opinions or show off their aficionado knowledge. In the case of wikis and blogs, the benefits are many and various—though rarely financial, measurable, or direct—and often involve self-expression and social connections. The payoff of my sharing the record of my listening habits via iTunes, my watching habits via Netflix, or my book ratings via Amazon is that I get higher-quality recommendations to help me discover new material that will excite me. In the case of several of the music services (with other media sure to follow soon), I can also match my listening profile with those of other fans who share my tastes, and make new friends.

Several of these services also support the tearable web. iLike (ilike.com) enables you very straightforwardly to display the songs you've listened to most recently on your MySpace profile. MOG encourages you to specify a set of songs you would recommend to others, which are shown on your MOG profile and can also be "torn" onto your blog or other online profile.

This ability to copy and paste segments of your data across the net shows the potential of modular services and technologies, which fans can remix to suit their purposes and adapt to meet fluctuating and uncertain demands. (And in the process it also acts as ambient advertising for the services themselves. Every visitor who sees the MOG recommendations on your personal profile is picking up not just the personal expression of your current favorites, but also the message that, hey, it might be cool to join MOG to make their own recommendations.)

Web 2.0

This basket of features and the potential they offer—the tearable web, the encouragement of personal expression and sharing, a people-centric organization of data, and the harvesting of individual data for both individual and collective benefit—has come to be known by the term "Web 2.0." In keeping with the disparate, modular nature of the concept, it has no hard-and-fast definition. But as with the concept of a game—for which there is also no hard-and-fast definition—this absence does not prevent us from using the term successfully and feeling reasonably confident about its application to a new breed of online developments.

The plug-and-play nature of the Web 2.0 platform does not end at sharing small modules of personal data, as demonstrated in the tearable web. The first era of the World Wide Web's growth was characterized by a race to gain "first-mover advantage." The idea was almost literally to lock in users by getting them to entrust their personal profiles and data to your service to such an extent that when a competitor service came on the scene, users would not want to transfer their loyalty—even if the new service was superior—because that would require them to start from scratch and re-enter all their data.

Web 2.0 does not do away with first-mover advantage. (Having invested in innovation, it's reasonable to expect businesses to enjoy some advantage as a result of getting there first.) But the ethos of Web 2.0 recognizes that the idea of owning all or most of the user's experience is a nonstarter on the net. To seek to lock in users in this way would require a predictability of demand and a docility among the audience that are no longer plausible. Providers in the Web 2.0 world aim to excel in providing specific services, while recognizing that their users will also be using other services and that *it's in the providers' interest* to make it easier, not harder, for the services to work together and for their users to move their data between them. Remember Jennings' law from Chapter 1: People make most of their discoveries elsewhere, which creates the incentive for discovery-oriented services to work seamlessly with other sites.

Take MyStrands and Last.fm, for example. Because Last.fm has licensed some of the data it has collected on personal listening profiles, you can use this data to extract more value from MyStrands.[102] On the MyStrands site, you enter your Last.fm username, and you can then extract a set of song suggestions based on MyStrands' recommendation engine. This is simply replicating what Last.fm could do, but based on a different set of data points. However, let's say you want to check out the MyStrands service to see if there are many other fans there who share your mix of tastes. Using your Last.fm profile data, MyStrands can give you a list of other MyStrands members with tastes similar to yours. The problem with joining a new online community used to be that you began with a "cold start": no profile, no contacts, and no straightforward way of making contacts. MyStrands' use of your Last.fm data helps overcome this hurdle.

It's an ethos that some commentators have called "winning by sharing,"[103] and it reflects a vision of a Web 2.0 platform where, instead of a handful of dominant communities with tens of millions of members, there would be thousands of communities, each with members in the thousands or tens of thousands. These communities would be oriented around niche and specialist interests, and you might be a member of several of them concurrently, carrying your relevant personal data with you as you rove round the net.

Thus this Web 2.0 version of the net accelerates the trends in discovery we've discussed earlier in the book. It makes it easier for free-range fans to forage widely, across diverse patches of online resources, picking up clues and recommendations as they go, and passing them on across different communities.

Blogs: Variety is the spice of life

...**If the first** wave of web development in the 1990s was characterized by a publishing model, the second wave is more like a scrapbook—though it's a scrapbook where others can share and comment on each element. Blogs, wikis, and social networking sites require fewer technical skills than web-page design used to, which means that many more people are now able to create web content. Overall, there is a loss of professional ethos—a quick tour of MySpace will show a bewildering and messy range of profiles and blogs, with an assault of different visual and aural elements—but what is lost in consistency is made up for in variety and independence.

We saw in Chapter 3 that roughly one in a hundred members of a community originates new material for that community, while one in ten modifies, synthesizes, or otherwise responds to that material. As simpler, more user-friendly tools for blogs and wikis come onstream, they create the potential to increase these levels of participation. They accelerate the spread of blog culture with its people-centric, authentic voices, and they increase the diversity of those voices.

A range of tools and services exists to enable people to create and share material, from reviews to photos taken at concerts, and from "fan club-exclusive" memorabilia to playlists and content samples for listening and trying out. What users will produce with them, no one can predict. Yes, there may be an ethos of amateurism about much of what they do, but the ease of sharing and the good-natured competition among friends and communities gradually encourages everyone to raise their game, add new features to their profiles, and improve their designs. And, make no mistake, the lack of commercial payoffs does not rule out excellence. The world of blogs and fan websites includes some stunningly beautiful designs, evocative writing, insightful criticism, and many incredibly comprehensive, lovingly maintained databases. These are the new temples of fan culture.

The self-motivated character and the diversity of blog culture embrace the different attitudes and behaviors of Savant, Enthusiast, and Casual fans. Casual fans don't have to participate if they don't want to, but can still benefit from the material produced by Savants and Enthusiasts. They may add an occasional comment, as well as some tags to help them manage their own collections of audio, video, and text. Often the providers of blogging and social networking platforms will recognize these tiers in levels of participation by users. The committed fans pay subscription fees for extra features and privileges, while more casual users have the option of a basic free service that carries more advertisements.

This diversity and independence come with advantages and disadvantages. One of the advantages is that the loose coupling of different blogs and communities allows opinions to develop and evolve more independently than they would through the mass media or through a more homogeneous network. Recall that if people arrive at their assessments independently and then you add all the assessments together, you can get a wisdom-of-crowds effect where all the eccentric ratings cancel each other out and you can distill some essence of accuracy. But if everyone bases their ratings of songs or films on what other people have already made into hits, you're more likely to get a herd mentality.

The disadvantage of all these diverse blogs and communities is that, if you want to add together all the assessments and ratings that relate to a particular band or film maker, say, it's not easy to do. For a new visitor to the "blogosphere," as many call it, the experience may feel like a virtual Tower of Babel with multiple voices talking past each other and only occasionally achieving collective coherence. While this is a issue that will never be solved once and for all, progress can be made, especially if more services on the Web 2.0 platform adopt common data standards to support sharing and aggregation. Technorati (www.technorati.com), for example, aims to help you browse and search across multiple blogs with the assistance of tags, to catch the pulse of the blogosphere on current issues. The Hype Machine (hypem.com) is an experimental service that tracks a huge number of blogs whose subject is music and which offer MP3 files for download. Using standard feeds from those blogs, it provides hour-by-hour updates on what tracks are being discussed on blogs, and what the most active and popular blogs are.

Rock 'n' roll: Attitude and appetite

...In the film *Wild at Heart*, Nicolas Cage plays a character with an Elvis Presley fixation and an obsessive attachment to his garish snakeskin jacket, which, he explains several times, is "a symbol of my individuality and my belief in personal freedom." This kind of rock 'n' roll attitude, the means of expressing it, and the volatile energy that Cage's character displays embody some of what drives the new era of word-of-mouth recommendations and exploratory free-range foraging.

First, then, rock 'n' roll is about personal expression. It's about speaking your mind, being straight and unreserved. This lack of pretense in relationships and exchanges in the new era is what Robert Scoble and Shel Israel call, in their book of the same name, "naked conversations."[104] At the same time, individual expression is often a way of expressing affiliation with a group of like-minded people, as in the tribal way that fans of a band or genre of music will gang together to outdo each other in articulating the reasons that another band sucks. This combination of individuality and group membership is one of the dynamics that drives social networking sites like MySpace, Facebook, and Bebo. The energy it creates is particularly strong among, but is not exclusive to, younger people.

Rock 'n' roll is anti-authority. In the film *The School of Rock*, Jack Black's character explains to his class of students how "the Man" is in charge, and how rock 'n' roll used to provide a way of fighting the Man, but, "guess what, oh no, the Man ruined that, too, with a little thing called MTV!"[105] This reflects a distrust of mainstream "old" media that is now channeled through the do-it-yourself ethos of blogs and wikis. A good dose of healthy skepticism is a useful antidote to bandwagon jumping and herd behavior. Rock 'n' roll keeps things moving. It lauds the new rebel on the block, but mocks them when they get a mainstream following. This guards against the sclerosis that infects many social institutions as they scale up and become established, and thereby encourages innovation. But is MySpace the new MTV?

Rock 'n' roll is about hanging out with the band backstage and getting the inside scoop on what's new and what's hot. Creative producers, from artists to authors and theater companies, have discovered the benefits of blogging as a means of lifting the veil on some of their behind-the-scenes work. They have found it a useful way of engaging with fans, building their loyalty, and encouraging them to spread the word to their friends. Facilitating this direct connection between artists and fans is undoubtedly one of the things that MySpace has executed particularly well. A lot of what its younger users do on the site could be classed as hanging out.[106]

While hanging out may seem like an undirected, intangible activity, communities like MySpace provide it with tangible measures (the comments and friends listed on your profile), a social currency that enables you to display how you're in with the in crowd. Add to this the potential not just to indicate which films and bands you like but *to have that respect reciprocated by the bands*—even if only in a token form, when they add you as a friend—and you see how the communities can accelerate the buzz around an exciting new band that is also a member of the community. The value of bands to you is not just in your enjoyment of their music and the ways you can project your identity by displaying your interest in them. Now the bands can actively help you in raising your status and making you look cool among your peers. By providing an incentive and social rewards for being among the first to make "friends" with emerging bands and artists, MySpace has reinvigorated the place of music in youth culture—and made discovering unsigned bands a hip thing to do.

Rock 'n' roll channels sexual energy. Dark Love (www.gothicsouls.com) is a dating website for goths. Its home page includes thumbnail profiles for several of its members. As well as a photo, each member lists a favorite book, film, song, and quote (*Interview with a Vampire* and *Lord of the Rings* feature strongly). Expressing your cultural tastes is often a central part of dating and mating rituals. The tagline of the MOG social networking service—"discover people through music and music through people"—captures the two-way street of discovery and relationships. You're attracted to people who share your tastes and interests, and you trust recommendations from people you like or to whom you are attracted. You can see how overlapping interests in music, film, or books can serve as an ideal, non-threatening icebreaker in making new friends online. And the dating site member who sees a photo of someone they like the look of, but isn't familiar with that person's favorite film or song, may feel a sudden urge to explore that material just to create the opportunity for such an icebreaker. Of course, only a minority are young, free, single, and active on the dating scene, but that doesn't stop the rest of the population from being motivated by the occasional frisson with friends and strangers.

Rock 'n' roll has a dark side. Originally it helped define a generation gap by being something parents really didn't want their children to get involved with. There are still moral panics about the risks young people may be taking in disclosing large amounts of personal information online, and potentially falling prey to predatory sociopaths. Dangers come in all shapes and sizes. The very openness and participative nature of Web 2.0 platforms make them vulnerable to interference from unscrupulous promoters. We've seen how some organizations will pay people to post messages online to support and promote their artists. They may also seek to bias rating systems by submitting favorable reviews of their clients, and to distort recommender systems by, let's say, setting up lots of dummy users who listen extensively to The Beatles and to the new band that they are promoting. That way the recommender systems will notice the correlation and encourage lots of Beatles fans to listen to the new band. This kind of activity is not new, especially in the music industry, where record labels would do whatever they could to secure radio play and high chart positions for their artists. With Web 2.0, however, the equivalent activities may be harder to detect and providers have to be forever watchful. As one commentator put it, the susceptibility of these technologies to being "spammed" is one of their defining features.[107]

I may be stretching the metaphor almost to breaking point here, but there is a yin and yang about rock 'n' roll in the way that, for all its devil-may-care abandon and improvisation, it relies on its opposite to sustain it. In other words, someone has to do the dull, glamor-free chores of making sure the band gets to the gig on time and the electricity is working when you plug in the guitars. In the Web 2.0 world, if the yang is the unrestrained flow of independent opinions across the net, then the yin that complements it is the canonical metadata that helps detect when people are talking about the same thing.

One of the problems that currently constrains the kind of profile sharing between Last.fm and MyStrands discussed above is that different systems have slightly different metadata for tracks and artists. Even small typographical or formatting inconsistencies in track titles can mean that although one system knows how many times I listened to a track, how I rated it, and how I tagged it, another system may not recognize what the track is, so my profile data is lost to it. While it's useful to have some data that is subject to continuous updating by anyone, as with descriptive tags and some Wikipedia details, it's equally important to be able to fix definitive versions of data that do not change, such as titles, creators, and dates.

The nonprofit MusicBrainz project aims to build a standardized and reviewed database of all music releases, and is one example of work to this end. It is complemented, in turn, by automated acoustic fingerprinting technologies that can recognize a sound file and then attach the right metadata. These are the kinds of Cinderella tasks that keep the show on the road and oil the wheels of the Web 2.0 tour bus.

Casting the net wider

...The next stop for Web 2.0 is to extend the reach of the net to the point where the world of bytes links up with the world of atoms, where internet technologies are embedded in everyday devices and locations. Cyberspace and the blogosphere will no longer be territories set apart from the real world and mainstream media; they will be part of them. Again, the emphasis is on accelerating the emerging trends among fans' habits that support discovery and exploration. We'll look at examples of this that help people to audition, meet, and mix in public spaces, that "socialize" the media, and that support the habits of collectors and Savants.

Imagine you're interested in going out to gigs and shows in your city, and meeting people there to share a drink and discuss the experience. While there are long-established local listings services to give you advance notice of who's playing where and when, the process of establishing which new bands might be worth seeing and who among your network of contacts might be interested in attending is long-winded. It's likely to involve not just the listings services, but hunting out band websites or MySpace profiles to try out their tracks, and then canvassing other people in your network of contacts via email or community sites. This overhead means that it tends to be only committed fans that make the effort.

The next generation of net services will draw together local and global data to reduce the effort required and make coordination easier. With Podbop (www.podbop.org), for example, you just need to enter your city and the service will find not just the listings of shows, but also MP3 versions of songs by the bands playing. If you subscribe to the feed at the site, you automatically receive a podcast of music by bands visiting your city, which you can listen to on a computer or iPod to find out which sound promising. What if you would like to get other recommendations for gigs and see who else is going? Last.fm will scan the local listings to alert you to gigs by artists that you have listened to a lot, as well as those that your friends are going to. You can see all the Last.fm members who are going to each gig, and possibly make new friends. With both Last.fm and Podbop adopting Web 2.0 approaches, it would be possible to develop a "mash-up" service that combines the data and functionality of both.

As discussed in Chapter 6, recommender systems have been developed as personalized services delivered to individuals who are more or less independent of each other in virtual space. MyStrands is the first to experiment with a hybrid, interactive music discovery service that brings recommendations into bars and clubs where you and your friends can register your requests and hear what amounts to a collaborative DJ set. You send requests and messages to the system using your mobile phone and these are displayed on a large screen. If you and any of your friends are MyStrands members, the service will take account of the preferences in your profiles and sift through the requests to find tracks that everyone in the group likes. This kind of collective filtering is still in its early stages, but in the future—as more mobile devices gain the ability to share song files across wireless networks—we can expect it to play a part in making the use of iPods and other digital players a much less individual and more social activity.

As well as social spaces, the net is reaching out to print and broadcast media. This is more a case of coexistence and convergence than colonization, since the established media have many characteristics that the internet cannot yet match. We are already seeing many cross-media packages, from CDs that come with "bonus" DVDs to boxed sets that are accompanied by extensive booklets. Music biographies and books of criticism are often published with tie-in CD releases compiling the music that soundtracks the book (after all, it's very frustrating to read someone rhapsodizing about an influential piece of music and not know what it sounds like).[108] Fans, meanwhile, are already creating their own soundtrack accompaniments to these books, using subscription services like Napster and Rhapsody, as well as other means of playlist sharing.

Entertainment magazines are extending their activities online, so that as well as a cover-mounted CD or DVD, they are offering net radio broadcasts and podcasts. Many have blogs on which readers can provide comment and feedback. However, few yet have the means for subscribers to tag, recommend, and comment on online versions of their articles and interviews in the way that you can with photographs on Flickr or tracks on MyStrands. Perhaps magazine content is not, as the new media jargon has it, sufficiently compelling on its own to draw and sustain the interest of large numbers of people. But a mature Web 2.0 platform should make it possible to integrate data across the net (along with relevant permissions to manage subscriber-only access), so that a new magazine interview with Bruce Springsteen can be automatically linked from Springsteen's biographical profiles in Wikipedia and Last.fm, along with some indication of its "interestingness" as measured by user comments and tags.

If Bruce Springsteen is also interviewed on the radio, then Web 2.0 should make it easier for foraging fans to discover the interview, and to home in on the most interesting parts. The BBC has been exploring ways to enable listeners to tag and annotate its programs with wiki-like features.[109] Listeners would also be able to decide how to subdivide the programs into sections. (At the moment this would require you to listen to the programs via a computer, but who knows whether the radios of the future will come with keypads and pointers to support these kinds of genuinely interactive features.) The idea is to use these listener contributions as an aid to navigation and search, helping people discover the specific elements of programming that are most relevant to their interests.

Many broadcasters will want their content to merge as seamlessly as possible into the conversation of bloggers and online communities, and this is likely to involve allowing their viewers or listeners to identify, at a fine-grained level of detail, the parts that interest them. As outlined in Chapter 6, the likes of MusicIP are building enormous databases such that every song on the radio (and even each performance of the song, whether it's a studio or live recording, or a cover version) could have its own unique identifying code. By hooking in to such databases, broadcasters could use Web 2.0 principles to offer radio listeners not just a simple tracklisting of their programs, but links to artist biographies, related videos, lyrics, discographies, and online retailing, as well as their own editorial input. Perhaps unsurprisingly, an experimental service called Sleevenotez (www.sleevenotez.com) already exists for Last.fm listeners. For each song you listen to, it collects much of this related material on one web page.

Matthew Shorter, interactive editor for music at the BBC, talks of "looking at the entire internet as the canvas on which the BBC has to work." Instead of expecting you to come and find it on the net, he wants BBC material to be available in the places you and your friends gather anyway, whether that's MySpace or Second Life or wherever else. Then, of course, once you have found that material, the BBC hopes to encourage you to visit its site from there.

What's on offer here is a means of tackling the infinite task of indexing all the world's media, and then of retrieving whatever text, audio, and video exists for presentation in the appropriate contexts, whether that's automatically linking to past Bruce Springsteen magazine and radio interviews from his biography, or alerting you to future live or broadcast performances.

Clearly, Savants and Originators are going to have a field day with all this potential. Fan communities that used to coordinate sharing of bootleg recordings through convoluted postal distribution, known as "tape trees," will be able to catalog all their resources and pool them virtually. In the case of live concert recordings for which artist permission has been given, this already happens through services like the Live Music Archive (www.archive.org/details/etree), but this practice will extend to interviews, reviews, features, and memorabilia. To make these objects easier to find and share, fans may tag them physically with Radio Frequency Identification tags, which help to track their location.

The endeavors of a committed few will accelerate the growth of comprehensive archives that provide rich pickings for free-range foraging fans and provide routes to deeper engagement with their favorite artists and stars.

Part V
Scenarios for the future

10

Future consumers:

Sharing experiences...

I n this final part of the book, we'll look at how the *Net, Blogs and Rock 'n' Roll* era will affect consumers, creators, and culture. The wave of dot-com-style excitement over the potential of Web 2.0 has given rise to a litany of media reinventions, from TV 2.0 to BBC 2.0, Learning 2.0, and even Books 2.0 and Music 2.0. The obvious "me too" bandwagon nature of this trend quickly becomes tiresome, and the terminology will surely become dated before very long. However, the common thread that links all these initiatives is that they take a medium as we know it (that is, "version 1.0") and add a layer made up of the techniques and technologies described in this book: tags and folksonomies, user contributions, the tearable web, and the three strands of digital discovery, Trying out, Links, and Community.

We hear of mass participation and the transition to "lean forward" media (contrasting with the "lean back" nature of most television consumption), and to understand the implications of these we need to take a closer look. Mass participation in the form of millions voting on *American Idol* or *Pop Idol* is one thing. But mass participation in the form of lots of us becoming Originators and Synthesizers in the niche areas of culture where our passions lie will have quite a different, and arguably more far-reaching, impact. As the example of Wikipedia shows, even minority participation on this model can produce significant resources to guide others' discoveries, given the right model for coordinating the energies of disparate individuals. Alternatively, if mass participation means experiencing our favorite music or television programs in the company of the friends in our social networks—even when they're in a different place—and swapping or tagging our favorite clips, then the impact will be different again.

Of course, mass participation in the fan economy involves all of these things and more. This chapter focuses on a range of scenarios of how we can share, use, discover, and explore entertainment. The next one looks at the issues for those in the business of being discovered and for those in the business of helping people make discoveries: of mediating between creators and consumers. The concluding chapter reviews the broader implications for our culture, including historical and global dimensions, and asks where we're heading.

Shared culture and the culture of sharing

...Will the combination of the enormous range of entertainment at our fingertips and the pocket-sized multimedia devices that are now widely available mean that we all consume personalized and idiosyncratic menus of culture in isolation from each other?

I hope it's clear by now that I don't subscribe to the theory that the new era of discovery will dissolve our social cohesion. On the contrary, it is providing us with new ways of connecting with friends and hooking up with strangers who share our interests.

A completely personalized culture would be like a private language: a contradiction in terms, and not much use to anyone. The increasing ubiquity of portable devices that absorb people's attention in public spaces may create the impression of a population retreating into cocoons; and Michael Bull's research with Walkman and iPod users (see Chapter 6) shows that cutting oneself off from the bustle of urban life *is* one of the motivations for using iPods and the like. However, with the spread of inexpensive wireless networks, these devices are sprouting more social features that encourage sharing and communicating between people, bringing them together rather than keeping them apart.

Perhaps it is straying too far into the realm of fancy to imagine that the commuter trains of the future will have one carriage for a "smart mob" holding an impromptu colloquium on recent developments in *Desperate Housewives*, while in the next carriage fans are sharing Green Day videos; though it could happen. We know that fans love to share and pass on their enthusiasm for their favorite audio and video stuff, and the new technologies will augment their ability to do so, at the time and place of their choosing.

Social impulses are central to blog culture, and often explicitly help in discovery. Take one of the conventions of blogging, for example. If you find an interesting story or site on someone else's blog and you decide to write about it on your own blog, it's common practice to mention where you found it and to provide a link back. This serves two purposes. First, it's a tip of the hat to the blogger who has pointed you to something worth exploring, a public gesture of thanks and respect. Second, it's a signal to the readers of your blog that if they're foraging for more interesting stuff, there's a good source over thataway. These two signals reinforce each other and strengthen the social glue of the blog community.

As blogs and social networks go mobile, this ethos will cross over from the net to the bars, concert venues, galleries, and cinemas where we meet old and new friends. Technology will catalyze these meetings and the decisions we make with these friends about where to go and what to see.

Let's say you're a film fan who takes a long weekend to visit a film festival. You're also a member of a social network where you've recorded ratings of films that you've seen and swapped comments about them with other members. Over time you've built a rapport with some of these fellow members and tagged them as contacts or friends. In the not-too-distant future, technology will enable you to see which of your contacts are also attending the festival, and, by logging in to the network via a pocket device with wireless net access, you'll be able to message them, call them, and (subject to privacy permissions) even see where they are and what they're doing at the festival at that moment. You and your friends will "flock" in small and larger groups, adapting your plans on the fly to get the right mix of catching the films you really want to see and getting together with others over a drink to chat about them.

Thus technology lubricates social interaction, and this interaction makes the cultural events more of a collective experience. With all of us having masses of data at our fingertips, you might imagine that we would all plan our leisure diaries some way in advance and with military precision. But most of us don't like to organize our social lives like our work and prefer more spontaneity. Social networks and mobile communications will make this possible by enabling us to coordinate with each other and switch between alternative plans at short notice.

For those who are single, or just outgoing, there is scope to turn each concert, each screening, and each gallery into a meeting place for like-minded people who have previously conversed only through the net.

Dynamic collections

...There may also be more spontaneity in the way we build and use our collections of music and other media in the digital age. Those in the recording industry who were at first concerned about the availability of free music on radio later came to see this as an ideal vehicle for promoting their product. Something similar seems to be happening with downloadable files, at least in the independent sector and the Long Tail, where there appears to be a recognition that you have to give a little, in the way of free samples, to get attention and interest, and to build an audience and a career.

So far only the committed fans, the Savants and Enthusiasts, have had the time and energy to keep track of all the promotional free downloads available on the net. But we can expect this to change as technologies to scan, index, and search— the future equivalents of sites such as the Hype Machine and tools like Songbird—become more powerful and more user-friendly.

Thus even Casual and Indifferent music fans may be able to accrue sizeable music collections, almost without meaning to. It will not just be a matter of pulling it off the net; email, messaging, and online feeds will also be used to push new music out into the world in search of an audience. This is the net equivalent of the CDs, DVDs, and games that come attached to the cover of a magazine. Whereas freebie CDs may get lost at the back of a cupboard and freebie downloads currently tend to languish in the marginal detritus of our hard disks, future generations of analysis and playlisting tools will help us all get more value from them.

Imagine a software application that "scrapes" the free tracks from multiple web pages, messages, and feeds without you even having to read them, and then organizes the tracks in relevant folders on your hard drive, based initially on artist and album data. Imagine that you can then instruct the application to compile a playlist of a certain length (to accompany a long train or bus journey, or a home video sequence, say). You specify whether you want it mostly up-tempo or downbeat, and what range of moods you are looking for. The application obediently searches your collection, and puts together a playlist that combines tracks in a sequence with just the right transitions of tempo and mood between them.

The science-fiction author Douglas Adams once envisioned, as a joke, a home robot that would watch all your unwatched video recordings for you. This was solely for the purpose of saving you the bother of having to watch them yourself. But the technologies that follow the Global Music Relationship Engine (see Chapter 6) will do more than just listen. They will automatically analyze tracks and assign a selection of useful tags accordingly, saving you the bother (though you will still be able to add your own tags, if you wish). They may be helped in this task by research work already under way at MIT's Media Lab to classify the emotional mood of songs automatically, based on their lyrics.[110]

One of the quips in the film *High Fidelity*, a romantic comedy set in the world of music junkies, was that spending an afternoon or two reorganizing your record collection could provide the necessary therapeutic solace at the end of a failed relationship. In the digital collections of the future it won't be just the Savants who have collections big enough to need careful organizing. However, reorganizing these collections will increasingly be done at the touch of a button, so it will be quicker and easier, but perhaps not so therapeutic. We won't need to think of music simply in terms of artist and album title, or of film and television solely in terms of lead actors and genre. Instead, we'll be able to choose among a much wider range of organizing factors, from mood to date of release, each of which can be invoked in an instant, with secondary sorting, if we want it, according to how frequently we've played each item. In this way we will build listening and viewing experiences that mix fresh material with old favorites, constituting a forever-morphing collection that provides a personalized radio-style service, similar in some ways to Last.fm and Pandora.

Tracking down music for casual hobbies

...**It is becoming** easier for everyone to use music and video in ways that were previously the domain of professionals and Savants, whether it's compiling a playlist on iTunes, having it done for you by a software application, or selecting something to accompany a home movie or liven up a jogging routine.

Even those who are more or less indifferent to music as a pastime sometimes create videos, presentation slides, or a personal profile on MySpace, all of which can be enhanced by some form of musical accompaniment, just as they will benefit from well-chosen pictures to illustrate particular ideas. So music and pictures that can be licensed freely or cheaply to complement their concepts or messages will be much in demand.

But when it comes to tracking down the right piece of music, searching with keywords often isn't the best solution, especially if you're not an expert. You may know the feeling when you can almost hear the kind of sound you want in your head, but you can't put into words the terms that would describe it. Savants may be masters at conjuring new terms like "jangly indie-folk" or "post-psychedelic chamber pop," but these are about as much use to the ordinary music listener as a dictionary of Ancient Greek. Much better to be able to identify a track that sounds something like what you have in your head, and then search for others that sound similar. (This is itself a classic foraging strategy: mixing instinct with technique, starting from a point that feels close to where you want to be, and then using all the means at your disposal to sniff out the best options from there.)

Imagine specialist music and media search services that help you work from your intuitions and guide you along paths that previous users have found fruitful. So if you want some music for your home video that sounds similar to a particular Madonna track but doesn't have the associated costs and licensing restrictions, you will be able to use that track as the "seed" for your search, and also refine the search to include only tracks that meet other criteria, including cost and ease of licensing.

But even with better search facilities and increased ease of use, hobbyists may still need to take advice from a more expert friend about some of the techniques and licensing implications involved in sourcing soundtrack music legally. As the law stands, it would be an infringement of copyright to take any music track, add it to a home movie, and then share the movie with even ten family members—unless permission has explicitly been granted. Some online video-sharing services use "sniffing" software to detect such infringements, and notify the perpetrators that they are in violation of their terms of service.[111] To avoid being caught out, you might want to restrict your search to work that creators have made available under Creative Commons licenses, which permit noncommercial uses without payment. Yahoo! already allows you to search the web for Creative Commons material, and its photo-sharing service, Flickr, enables you to find Creative Commons photos, which many bloggers use to add visual interest to their writings.

Teenage kicks

...While rock 'n' roll, movies, videos, and games are no longer the preserve of hormone-driven teenagers, it's still in the first flush of youth that passions for these forms of entertainment and culture are fired, affiliations are forged, and habits take hold, some of which may last a lifetime. So it's no surprise that everyone from media empires to regulators and educators shows a close interest in how young people are adapting to the digital, always-connected world. Several commentators and futurists argue that the generation born after

1985 have only ever known the interconnected world of the net
and mobile communications, and that as a result, their approach
to media as "digital natives" is qualitatively different from that of
older generations. We will have to wait until 2020 to find out
whether the digital natives carry these differences through to
their mid-30s, and whether a new generation gap opens up
behind them as they become the Establishment and approach
middle age. But there are some characteristics of each generation
of young people that have held true for some time in western
democracies:

> ... By comparison with older generations, they are rich in
> time and poor in money.
> ... They are preoccupied with their social standing among
> peers, tending to aggregate in small clusters and
> sometimes divide along almost tribal lines.
> ... They frequently use music and other popular culture as
> a system of signifiers to help them explore their
> identities, their sexuality, and their values.

We're used to the idea—and the alarm it causes in some
quarters—that young people's early experience of acquiring
music and video is that they share it for free via the net. Up until
recently, this illicit activity has at least been tethered to
computers, which, as they are relatively expensive and fragile
devices, are often overseen (if only indirectly and occasionally) by
adults. As it gets increasingly easy to swap files using mobile
phones and cheap digital music players with wi-fi networking
capabilities, young people's sharing will become even more feral.

The question is whether, rather than striking fear into
the heart of the music industry, this trend could be turned round
to create new opportunities. This would depend, first, on finding
an alternative way to compensate creators for the use of their
work. But then, if the industry's emphasis were to switch from

controlling such sharing behavior to monitoring and reporting on it, kids' attitudes could be subtly molded at the same time as their energies are being tapped. Everyone knows that having young people evangelize about their favorite bands is good for those bands' development. In the UK, Universal Records used to run a scheme to encourage young fans to become "school chairmen" and distribute promotional material for bands like Busted and McFly to their schoolmates in return for free merchandise. The scheme was suspended following a newspaper investigation.[112] Instead of these cloak-and-dagger operations by both industry and fans, why not bring fan evangelism out into the open, measure it, and provide charts of the top fans, so that the election of "chairmen" can be seen to be done on merit?

Perhaps kids' chart position in the Top 40 Fans might be based on the number of times they have played their favorite band's tracks, combined with how many comments they have added to the band's profile on a social networking platform, and the number of people with whom they have shared the tracks. Since young people's movements tend to be restricted to a few neighborhoods, these charts could be highly localized, perhaps down to specific zipcode areas. This would give the kids a real sense of involvement, enabling them to measure themselves against people they know in school or college, and to see the impact of their own behavior as they go up and down the charts of different artists, week by week. The music industry would benefit in that the localization would give it pinpoint accuracy on how the buzz about an artist emerges first in one area and then spreads. It would help it to target promotional campaigns and live performances.

By giving tangible and measurable evidence of fans' commitment to their favorite artists, these charts would tap into the tendency that young people have to use their taste in music as a way of marking their individual and social identities. If being a "friend" of a band on MySpace gives a youngster the sense of a special and personal bond with its members, how might that be amplified if there is a clear "pecking order" of local fans? Teenagers will strive for the prestige of being among the first to latch on to the hot new bands and to help their cause by sharing their tracks with as many people as possible. Bands might give further incentives for such behavior by making available the kind of merchandise offered by the Universal Records' scheme, and even backstage passes to their top fans when they visit the area. But even without such incentives, young people's desire for status among their peers will drive them to spread the word.

Parents may come to resent such behavior, of course. Picture the scene when young Tracy asks for a lift to a nearby neighborhood, and it gradually dawns on her mother that the real motive for this trip is to evangelize for Tracy's favorite boy band and share their latest song with a different group of peers, just to improve her chart rating as a fan. Cue some exasperated parental tut-tutting, along with concerns that Tracy is being exploited as an unpaid promotional agent.

Creating and curating the archive

...Online fan resources are a very mixed bag, and that's the way they will always be. Some are knocked together in a few hours and then forgotten, while others are forever works in progress. Three things will raise the bar for these amateur shrines. One will be the fans' adoption of increasingly sophisticated technology. Another will be the competitiveness of some of the most dedicated fans: the Originators we met in Chapter 3, who have invested all their spare time in building beautiful sites, and can be almost as zealous as teenagers about keeping their work out in front of that of others in the same field (especially if they *are* teenagers).

But more frequently than competition, it is collaboration that improves fan resources. The wiki approach may not lend itself to the "shrine" kind of fan site that expresses one person's devotion to an artist, but it fits well with the situation where you have a disparate group of volunteers who can spare just a bit of time now and then. On a wiki, it doesn't take long to create a page that, for example, lists the credits for an album or film. You can complete the bits you know, but leave it unfinished for others to add further details, or maybe create another page, linked from the first, that profiles the producer.

Blogs, too, can have multiple authors, and in the coming years we will see many more net-based services that incorporate wiki and blog features, along with collaboration tools to help coordinate the efforts of a range of volunteers. The groupware and workflow management technologies that were first developed for corporate environments are gradually migrating to the more open ethos of the net.

When dealing with collective volunteer effort, one pattern that emerges is that, by and large, people tend not to devote their time to maintaining resources about very popular items like reviews of *Titanic* or *Sergeant Pepper's Lonely Hearts Club Band*. They know that these are very popular titles, so they assume that other people will deal with these tasks. Instead, volunteers are more likely to focus on the specific areas where they feel they can make a contribution that few others would be able to make. Also they are motivated to create material that they think other people like them (with similar interests and attitudes) will value. Imagine being a member of such an informal fan community, where the technology tracks the tasks toward which you gravitate and, on the basis of this, automatically provides suggestions for further tasks that may be matched to your knowledge and aptitudes.[113] This could affect how you direct your time in the future—you may avoid proofreading a wiki page lest further similar tasks be suggested to you.

In future, if they're not already, fan communities will quickly become the most authoritative archivists for the artists they follow. They collect memorabilia and ephemera, from ticket stubs to magazine interviews and amateur bootleg recordings, that most people would dismiss as tat. Professional archivists, and the artists themselves, often have neither the means nor the mindset to store things that were never meant to last, and record labels and other media producers do not see such items as part of their intellectual property portfolio. A 1966 acetate version (which will not stand repeated playing) of a Velvet Underground LP attracted bids of over $100,000 on eBay 40 years later.[114] At present these artefacts are spread through the attics and cellars of a diaspora of fans, some of whom are still active while others are more or less lapsed. Future generations of wikis and blogs will provide the ideal collaborative platform to catalog each of the items, creating an incredibly rich resource for research and discovery.

As well as memorabilia, these items will include what are currently rare and hard-to-find audio and video recordings, which will be collected by both human foraging and automated "sweeping" of the net. Expert fans will catalog them and record their digital fingerprints, to help identify whether further discoveries are duplicates or new additions to the archive.

When they have shared concerns, fan communities may also morph into the digital-era equivalents of unions and guilds and coordinate lobbying or collective bargaining activities. When word got out that Epic Records was blocking the release of Fiona Apple's album *Extraordinary Machine*, fan sites such as FreeFiona.com sprang up to protest to the record label and petition it to release the album. The fans eventually got their way when a reworked version of the album was released several months later. Henry Jenkins, an MIT professor who has studied fan cultures extensively, cites similar cases of groups mobilizing to lobby for the broadcast of unaired television series or the extension of film franchises, and notes, "fans are starting to win more and more battles."[115]

Our data, our rewards

...**You have probably** spotted that one of the threads that runs through the scenarios in this chapter and earlier parts of the book is that computers and service providers are collecting ever more data about you: what you listen to and watch, how you rate and tag it, who your friends are, and what opinions you express to them. It is natural that you will want to control who has access to this information, how they use it, and how you can change it or move it about.

In the first wave of personalized online services, companies openly collected profile data from customers as a way of tailoring those services to them and, in the process, discouraging them from moving to other providers (who lacked the profile data). But if we ourselves contribute the data that enables personalization, shouldn't we own it and be able to choose which providers can access it? New services are springing up all the time and, as the best new ones leapfrog existing ones in which we have invested our time and data, we won't want to have to rebuild those profiles of most frequently played tracks and reapply tags to videos in our collection.

In Chapter 9 we saw how Web 2.0 techniques mean that you can draw on your Last.fm profile to get recommendations from within MyStrands. Possibly for commercial reasons, these providers don't currently let you export your data in a format that could be imported directly into other services. You can't easily take your purchase history and ratings on Amazon and use them to get a better quality of service from Barnes and Noble. However, Eric Schmidt, the CEO of Google, recently indicated his company's intent to avoid such protective practices, saying, "The more we can... let users move their data around, never trap the data of an end user, let them move it if they don't like us, the better."[116] It remains to be seen how many providers will follow suit, but some are already collaborating to create standards to

give you more control over your "attention data," the profile of
things you read, listen to, and watch.[117]

Openness and transparency will again be the best
strategy for the service providers involved. As Last.fm's Martin
Stiksel told me:

> We collect data about the music you listen to, and
> we make no bones about that fact: people can see
> it in the personal charts we provide on everyone's
> public profiles, so they come to *expect* it and to
> enjoy the benefits that the data bring.

Indeed, one of the uses of the data that Last.fm collects is to
provide charts of "top listeners" for each artist. There is no doubt
that some Last.fm members, like the young fans discussed earlier
in this chapter, covet inclusion in the upper reaches of these
charts, and may increase their listening to their favorite artists
accordingly, simply as a badge of their love.

Users are generally happy for certain types of personal
data to be published as long as their privacy is protected—and is
seen to be protected. When the Facebook social network
redesigned its service so that it was easier to track when other
people posted new journals or photos, users rebelled, claiming
that it made it too easy for people to indulge in stalker behavior.
Facebook pointed out that the new features did not disclose any
information that was not previously available, but merely
facilitated tracking of updates. That's not the point, came the
response from the users. Facebook quickly had to back down and
remove the new features.[118]

Users are also more sensitive if personal data seems to be
collected by stealth. Take the example of data about your music-
listening habits. Paradoxically, when Last.fm, MyStrands, and
iLike openly display data such as your personal charts and most
recently played tracks, this seems to create an impression of

straight dealing by the organizations concerned. It may also be that the net-savvy music fans who are the early adopters of such services realize that these organizations are independent players whose main business is building a community around their services, and that they are unlikely to have any ulterior motive for collecting this data.

By contrast, users were much more wary when Apple first started to collect the same data. Apple's MiniStore feature, introduced in early 2006 as part of its popular iTunes media player software, collected this data in order to recommend tracks to buy that were similar to those the user was listening to. This is very similar to the functionality provided by Last.fm and MyStrands, and Apple did not publish any user charts. But initially the MiniStore feature was switched on by default, and privacy-sensitive bloggers raised an alarm about personal music-playing data being passed back to Apple without users being aware of what was being collected.[119]

As with the Facebook case, Apple was pressured into altering the feature so that it was switched off by default and into issuing assurances that no data was tracked or collected in this state. To some degree, all this comparison does is demonstrate a case of mishandled communication. But there is also a general suspicion toward "big media" and "big science" interests such as Apple, particularly on the part of opinion-forming early adopters of advanced online services. The crowdsourcing model that underpins Web 2.0 services like Flickr, Wikipedia, Google, and Last.fm depends on us providing our personal information—our tags, usage data, content, and opinions—for free, while the service providers exploit this same information for revenue generation and commercial advantage. Most of us will accept the contract that use of our data is the price we pay for what is otherwise low-cost access to the services that give us better access to our own and others' photos, convenient reference sources, better search results, and effortless playlisting.

However, the dedicated Originators among us occupy a slightly different position. In the business world there are cases of people starting blogs as a sideline and ending up running them as full-scale businesses.[120] Many of those committed to documenting their favorite music and video may eschew opportunities for serious revenue generation. For example, Andy Aldridge's Galaxie 500 site earns him some money via Amazon's affiliate program (he gets a small commission on any sales at Amazon that are referred from his site), but not enough to cover his direct costs for hosting the site.[121]

However, some fan economy endeavors are approaching the status of cottage industries, and have a high profile in their niche areas. They may play a significant role in charting parts of the Long Tail that mainstream media fail to reach. Commercial interests may want to license the materials that fans have curated and created. If this happens, or if what fans have built directly helps to lift artists and creators—tomorrow's Vashti Bunyans— out of the Long Tail to reach a larger audience, they may be justified in expecting a nontrivial share of the earnings that result.

This is the point where the fan economy bleeds into the traditional media economy. There may be opportunities for some Originator fans to go semiprofessional if they show that they can build a credible audience or network of other fans, sufficient to attract sponsorship or merchandising deals. This could become a popular route to starting or building a career in the wider media sector, but it will also cause friction and disagreements where it is perceived to threaten the noncommercial ethos of hardline blog culture.

To sum up, then, the consumers of the future will have the means to behave even more like selfish, opportunistic scavengers if that's what they want. But the combination of their enthusiasms and the new digital possibilities will also lead them into deeper relationships with the material they like, while enhanced communications will draw them into richer connections with each other, whether that's hooking up with friends to share common interests or stimulating each other to explore new material. As bigger parts of our lives become visible online, the risks to privacy increase, yet so do the opportunities to produce truly exceptional material for other fans and would-be fans. Driven more by commitment and community than by commerce, the work they produce will add much to the rich weave of resources for discovery.

11

Future media: Designing for discovery

I n 1963, the Nobel prize-winning physicist Richard Feynman gave a series of lectures that presented a scientist's perspective on a range of societal and political issues. Referring to the US Constitution, he said:

> The government of the United States was developed under the idea that nobody knew how to make a government, or how to govern. The result is to invent a system to govern when you don't know how.[122]

In this book I have identified many factors that influence discovery. But that is not the same as saying that we can predict how anyone will make a particular discovery. So can we invent a system to help in discovery when we don't know how? And if we can, what freedoms should we inscribe, what powers should we grant to individuals, and what checks and balances, if any, do we need to regulate developments?

Arguably, the only principle that doesn't inhibit progress in discovery is "anything goes."[123] The infrastructure of the net, the spontaneous expression of blog culture, and the serendipitous nature of discovery itself mean that no one has control; everyone's power is finite. Consequently, there is no panacea, no magic bullet, to solve the "problem" of discovery. The overriding issue is to do everything we can to make certain that diverse routes of exploration continue to be available, and to avoid closing off any forms of discovery. This chapter addresses the challenges for those that make discovery their business, whether they are the creators wooing the consumers, or the intermediaries matchmaking between these two groups.

Creating shared experiences:
The new breed of smart intermediaries

...**One of the** predictions made in the early days of the World Wide Web was that it would bring about the end of intermediaries who got in the way of direct links between creators and consumers. But rather than being obliterated, these intermediaries are being transformed. Audiences and fans need them to make sense of the abundance of stuff that is out there fighting for our attention. Recommender systems, social networks, and blog culture are new and emerging solutions to this problem, and everyone from specialist magazines to mobile telecoms providers is getting in on the act.

However, the incumbent mainstream media still play the predominant role in discovery at present. In the UK, independent research carried out in 2006 asked more than 3,000 people to identify the two main means by which they found out about new music. Traditional radio dominated the responses, being named by 60% (along with 5% each for digital radio and internet radio), followed by music television, which was identified as a source by 42% of the survey group.[124] Compared with these figures, those for social networking sites like MySpace and Bebo were much more modest at 4% overall. The survey data show that these sites, along with blogs, podcasts, and other forums, are indeed very influential for those that use them; so far, though, that only counts for a minority, concentrated in younger age groups. For the time being, some forms of radio and television are likely to remain an important part of the discovery mix.

Net technologies and blog culture augment these media rather than replacing them. They provide the means to reconnect fans and audiences who are rarely listening to or watching the same thing at the same time now that so much is available. The new breed of smart intermediaries will look for ways to exploit this potential by recreating shared experiences for consumers, and enriching those experiences by adding contextual information and opportunities to communicate or contribute.

Take the case of a television listings service. On the face of it, it looks as though they will find themselves between a rock and a hard place, as the scope for free-range viewers to forage across multiple guides in search of their viewing options increases. They already have to compete with electronic program guides that are built into the television service, and with newspaper listings. Further competition may come from the fan economy. If production companies put trailers or sample episodes on YouTube, then bloggers can embed these in their homespun "picks of the week." Services like Tape It Off The Internet envisage a world where everything is available on demand, and listings are rendered redundant. Will services like the UK's *Radio Times* (established in 1923, before there were television programs to list, but one of the first to provide data to your personal digital assistant, turning it into a remote control for your television) be able to evolve still further to meet these challenges?

One way to add value to listings is to personalize them to the individual interests of each viewer. But increasing degrees of personalization come at the cost of retaining shared experience. If listings services are to survive, they may need to balance out the atomization of programming and of audiences by providing ways to re-aggregate the "atoms" into something that's coherent and greater than the sum of its parts. They won't recreate channels in the old sense, but through social networking and blogs they can bring together groups of viewers who share, watch, and discuss playlists of programs. One of the ways in which listings providers could catalyze these shared experiences would be through the combination of viewer participation and editorial filtering that *The Guardian* has demonstrated with its weekly music lists (see Chapter 5). By facilitating this participation and enriching the audience's engagement with what they watch, as well as with each other, new television services could create a truly premium viewing experience.

Ask the audience

...**The way forward** for intermediaries that produce audio, video, and print is to make sure that they are part of the tearable web, and to make it easier for their output to be woven into blog culture. The new generation of services such as YouTube and Last.fm are harbingers of this trend. And Mark Thompson, Director General of the BBC, demonstrates how this thinking can be applied in established media organizations when he speaks of a second wave of digital impact, following the first wave of the net and interactive television. The fundamental features of this second wave will include "more radical interaction, content generation and the pooling and sharing of that content across communities."[125] That the owners of MySpace immediately responded to this vision by accusing the BBC of wanting to create a rival to their service[126] shows that there will be a broad contested territory where public and commercial services, along with online and broadcast models, converge.

How these intermediaries develop relationships with, and among, their audience will be crucial. Indeed, even the language they use to describe this audience community will be symbolic. Consumers? That seems inadequate to describe a potentially more participative relationship. Members? That captures participation, but may create expectations of accountability and rights that come with membership, and intermediaries would have to be confident that they could meet such expectations.

The term "crowdsourcing" was coined to refer to the model of co-opting voluntary effort to help with tasks like rating, tagging, or developing wikis and community forums.[127] This model will become increasingly important to intermediaries that are seeking to support discovery. However, to work successfully, it depends on building trust with the intended participants, and referring to them as a "crowd" may incite the less constructive aspects of crowd behavior.

Many intermediaries will seek to encourage greater participation on the part of their audiences, not just so they can tap their knowledge and opinions, but also to develop deeper relationships and a sense of ownership or membership.

When television or radio networks commission new programs in future, they may expect producers to provide the material in a form that has already been audience tested and "seeded" with metadata (the tags, credits, and comments that describe the attributes the audience finds useful). Producers will identify communities of fans who are knowledgeable in the relevant area, and will invite them to tag and comment on each section of the material. Sometimes those comments might lead the editors to reorganize the material, or even alert them to other archive material they didn't know about—but it will also mean that when the program is first broadcast there are already some seed tags and markers there for the audience to browse and search on, which will take them further on their journey of discovery. This will make for a richer experience for the wider audience, who will increasingly expect to be able to skip forward and backward through broadcast programs, guided by tags through the content of each section. They will also be able to add new tags, of course.

A side-effect of this tagging could be a reduction in the value of pirated copies, assuming that these copies lack the tags and other metadata that the originals have (just as a photo downloaded from Flickr is not so useful when it no longer has the tags and comments attached to it when viewed on the Flickr site).

In future, intermediaries may provide their users with myriad ways to contribute to, and communicate through, their services, reflecting the range across the audience from Savants to Indifferents and from Originators to Lurkers. At one end of the spectrum the form that involvement takes may be relatively passive, such as when you provide data about the television programs you've been watching and you receive personalized recommendations in return. At the other end will be initiatives such as Al Gore's Current TV, which encourages viewers to make their own nonfiction videos for broadcast. Many of us seek different levels of involvement in different areas or at different times. For example, I may strive to keep at the head of the curve in some music genres and contribute daily to favorite radio programs, while just following critical and word-of-mouth wisdom about the best television and films to watch, participating only minimally, if at all.

Alongside user-generated media, there will still be a place for professionals with a strong and individual authorial voice. Consider the film footage taken by Timothy Treadwell, the self-appointed guardian of wild bears in Alaska, which was featured in the documentary *Grizzly Man*. The director, Werner Herzog, edited half the film from 100 hours of Treadwell's own footage. The other half comprised new material and interviews, shot by Herzog, which put Treadwell's footage in context, providing a critical assessment of his life's work and how it ended up killing him. Could the original footage have been put directly on YouTube, leaving a loose collective of viewers with diverse tastes and interests to rate and arrange it? At least one film critic has suggested that if Treadwell were alive and filming today, he might have bypassed other directors and gone straight to YouTube.[128] Perhaps he might, but I doubt that the viewers' experience would have been better for it. Arguably, they would have been able to draw their own conclusions about Treadwell, his motives, and his state of mind. But Herzog transforms the raw material by putting it in context, giving insights into Treadwell's blindspots with testimony from his acquaintances, lingering on shots that he felt Treadwell might have cut, and leaving no doubt about how his own view of nature and wild bears differs from Treadwell's. This authorial voice, the portrait it paints, and the argument it makes contribute to a story that holds the attention, informs, and stimulates for over 100 minutes. It's a full meal, rather than the kind of grazing you might do on YouTube clips.

Ultimately, however, it will be consumers who decide which version they want to watch. The media will make all the options available and leave it up to the audience to choose. This gives creators and producers a broad scope in their choice of business models. Do you go for the low-overhead, low-return options of using YouTube, MySpace, and Garageband.com, or get the budget that requires cinema and secondary revenues to break even? Do you pitch to be commissioned by one of the major radio networks, or make your own podcasts and sell subscriptions? As a creator, the choice is yours. And one may lead to the other.

The discovery triangle: Courting rituals

...There's a triumvirate of forces circling each other in the discovery game: consumers, creators, and intermediaries. In the age of file sharing, consumers are often portrayed as modern-day Don Juans, eager for quick conquest but wary of commitment.

While some of them no doubt conform to this stereotype, we've seen that there's considerable variation between those who are casual and those who are deeply committed.

To maximize their chances of being discovered and building a relationship with an audience, creators have to play a flirtatious game with consumers. They need to show just enough of themselves to entice consumers but still leave them wanting more, in the hope that they will commit to a serious relationship. Between creators and consumers, intermediaries play a complex range of roles from matchmaker to referee and score keeper.

Creators have to pitch their flirting correctly, striking a balance between on the one hand making their material sufficiently accessible to give themselves a good chance of attracting consumers, and on the other hand not making it so accessible that it undermines sales and revenues.

How and where to strike this balance differs between media formats. In music, for example, most creators are willing to let consumers hear a full song at least once, if not more, as an enticement for them to buy. A similar approach will not work for films, as access to a full film might decrease rather than increase the chances of a purchase. The science-fiction writer and eminent blogger Cory Doctorow explains the current state of play when it comes to electronic books:

> Mostly, we can read just enough of a free e-book to decide whether to buy it in hardcopy—but not enough to substitute the e-book for the hardcopy. Like practically everything in marketing and promotion, the trick is to find the form of the work that serves as enticement, not replacement.[129]

We're starting to see a new ecology emerging among creators, which divides along the lines of how far they are prepared to go with their enticements, how flirtatious they are. At one end of the spectrum are the do-it-yourself hobbyist or semiprofessional creators. As the saying goes, when you've got nothing you've got nothing to lose, so the DIY creators can act like promiscuous bohemians, putting out their material for all-comers to download and share with their friends. They don't mind if word gets out that they're "easy"—as long as word gets out. (Most bloggers are themselves exactly this kind of DIY creator.)

At the other end of the spectrum, the major record labels and studios are more cagey and coy. Rather than revealing significant parts of the work itself as enticement, they have budgets for marketing and promotion to give consumers the come-on. If they do give away any of the work, it tends to be wrapped in the chastity belt of Digital Rights Management software, which prevents consumers from doing some of the things they'd like to with it. But then, having invested significantly more in making their work compared with the DIY creators, they do have more to lose.

If rights owners won't relinquish control by licensing material to others, they could become media organizations themselves and seek to insert their material in a wider conversation that way. Some major labels, independent labels, and music publishers provide podcasts that expose their material,[130] but it's too early to say how widespread this provision may become.

The role artists themselves play in revealing more of themselves and their work to stimulate interest varies depending on what stage their career is at and the amount of recognition they can take for granted. But whether mainstream media are beating a path to an agent's door begging for an interview or the artist is just starting a blog on a social networking site, the challenge is to find a way of presenting themselves and what they're about in a way that will engage their target audience and make them want to find out more.

Some will approach this by devising a gimmick, a *succès de scandale* that ignites gossip, or a fairytale story that generates a buzz and catches the attention of other media channels. Not all artists will want, or be able, to go down one of these routes. But they can still engage interest by enticing potential fans "backstage" to learn more about them, and by offering occasional glimpses behind the veil to show their creative process. Blogging provides a natural and very low-cost means for artists of all kinds to do this. Many creative people keep notebooks and records of their ideas anyway, and they all have a passionate interest in others' work as well (having frequently been inspired to take up their chosen career by being fans of other people in the first place). So it's no surprise that the world of blogs is packed with articulate insights, reviews, and reflections from independent writers, film makers, musicians, and performers.

Blogging is by no means the only technology for lifting the veil on the creative life and providing resources for deeper connections between fans and artists. The Canadian band Cowboy Junkies produced a CD called *Anatomy of an Album*, which, "through words, pictures, lyric drafts and music, will take you down to the cellular level of each song off of the *One Soul Now* CD."[131] The parallel practice of providing a "making of" feature with the DVD release of a film to document the creative process is now well established. Artists may soon be distributing these multimedia diaries online as a means of inviting the audience a little further into their world and building a deeper bond with them.

Reasons to be wary: The fault line between creators and intermediaries

...Social networks like MySpace and Bebo have fanned the interest in emerging music artists, just as YouTube has either stimulated or uncovered an appetite for short video clips.

Along with interactive television shows like *American Idol* or *Pop Idol*, these new intermediaries have revitalized the experience of taking part in the discovery of new talent.

This new breed of intermediaries like creators who are prepared to be flirtatious with consumers. Social networks and portals such as Yahoo! will actively encourage creators to "put out" a bit more. The more they put out, the more material there is to circulate through the social networks and blogs, and this helps to draw in more consumers.

For their part, however, many creators are wary about the intermediaries' role. They resent the fact that the social networks are profiting, via subscriptions and advertising revenue, by providing a service that depends in part on their work. Perhaps the recording industry, film and television studios, and publishers could be more relaxed about this if they could see that the growth of blogs, social networks, and recommender systems was increasing their sales and decreasing their risks, including those arising from file sharing. The trouble is that they can't.

The interest stimulated by the likes of MySpace, Last.fm, and YouTube does not yet seem to translate directly into increased revenues for the creator industries as a whole. Many factors complicate this relationship. One may be file sharing, which is itself both an indicator of interest and, to a disputed extent, a drain on revenue. Then there are other general market factors including the growing competition between leisure media (music, video, games, plus mobile and online communities themselves) for a share of our time and disposable cash, and the related downward pressure on prices. Lower prices may mean that creators sell more DVDs or downloads, for example, but still see total revenues falling.

So creators crave extra routes that will lead their audience to them, and there's no doubt that case studies of how fans first discovered, say, Lily Allen or Hawthorne Heights through MySpace are exciting to the industry in their own way.[132]

But if they get the sense that any of the new breed of intermediaries are "taking advantage" of the creators' work—by not doing enough to detect and prevent copyright infringement, for example—it won't take much for them to withdraw their material and their cooperation. Witness, for example, the $1 billion legal action taken by television and movie conglomerate Viacom against YouTube for allegedly playing fast and loose with the former's television shows. This is symptomatic of a fault line between creators and rights owners on the one hand and intermediaries on the other.

Policing social networks

...**It's hard for** anyone to predict what the shape of the social networking market will eventually be. Possibly activity will concentrate around a handful of global sites, which would be much larger than MySpace, Bebo, and Facebook currently are. Alternatively, if Web 2.0 platforms and techniques take off sufficiently to enable people to transfer relevant parts of their profile and "friends" data between multiple sites, there could be a diverse archipelago of smaller social networks, each catering to niche interests like different genres of music or film. In all likelihood this isn't a case of either/or. Both large and small social networking sites will coexist, and many of us will participate in both kinds to differing degrees.

Whatever shape this growth takes, some changes in the character of social networking are inevitable. As the dirt roads become highways and the villages grow into cities, we are already losing some of the early innocence of online community building. Several bloggers report receiving death threats, and MySpace—created as "a place for friends"—has attracted scrutiny for exposing young people to predators and pedophiles. The disciplines required to tackle these challenges may not be those of the traditional business manager or engineer so much as the gardener, architect, or politician.

Social networks and other intermediaries will have to balance conflicting demands to provide opportunities for promotion and also be seen to be even-handed and unbiased. Choosing what to measure, how to measure it, and how to interpret and respond to the results will be critical.

For example, as competition heats up between social networks, savvy record labels and film studios will look beyond the headlines about Lily Allen before they sign up to providing the kind of exclusive previews of new material that R.E.M. did with MySpace. They will want hard figures showing the kinds of exposure they can expect from each social network, and the prospects for conversion into intermediate results ("friends," additions to mailing lists, or promotional clubs) and sales.

Businesses who buy advertising on websites already expect such data, and their payments are often tied to particular metrics for results. Creators may follow the advertising model when they come to do business with intermediaries; in other words, they will pay for placement—on prominent pages, in search results, or in playlists. When record companies pay for placement on radio playlists, it's known as "payola" and often causes a scandal. The objection to payola in the past was that it biased access to limited-exposure opportunities (that is, airtime on the finite number of radio stations that played new music) in favor of established companies who could afford to pay. In the *Net, Blogs and Rock 'n' Roll* era, exposure opportunities are no longer limited—if the radio blocks one of your routes to an audience, you find another route—so objections to payola in this new context arguably should fall away. Payola is still illegal in traditional radio, but online intermediaries are not subject to the same regulations.

Often no money changes hands with these inter-mediaries, but the creators "put out" a bit more in return for placement favors. Apple's iTunes Store offers creators placement on its main page in exchange for exclusive new songs, discount pricing, or additional material such as artist interviews.[133] On Last.fm, artists and record companies that provide MP3 versions of their songs for free download from the site will see their songs recommended more frequently on its interactive streams of music. There is a straightforward and open trade here. In return for providing an additional benefit that Last.fm can market to potential members, the record companies get more exposure for their artists. It may become increasingly common for interactive music and video services to feature "sponsored plays" of material, in the same way that web search engines like Google feature sponsored links alongside the rest of their search results.

Charting the celestial jukebox

...**Both creators and** consumers will also take an increasingly close interest in the charts that the new intermediaries produce, and how they regulate them. Again, there will be conflicting pressures from different interests. As we saw in Chapter 4, the traditional sales-based charts are being undone by the complexities of digital convergence and the multiple offerings it provides, yet charts based instead on numbers of plays lack movement and drama. A number of possible solutions to these issues are emerging, many of them focused on producing measures and charts that are more effective filters for discovery.

To overcome the lack of drama in the main charts, some intermediaries are publishing charts based on more sophisticated measures, which may help identify the Next Big Thing. The BBC's 6 Music radio station broadcasts an album chart that specifically excludes any band or artist that has ever had a Top 40 hit in the main album chart. It does this to weed out mainstream and established hits and focus more on emerging and marginal music.

As MySpace has become a *de facto* platform for promoting and discovering new bands, artists and managers have touted its measures as signs of their popularity—look how many friends we've got, look how many times our songs have been played. Referring to these measures is a nod to the supposed wisdom of crowds, and to the logic that says that, if a band or film has already attracted attention and support, it must be good, and it must stand a good chance of attracting more of the same.

The trouble with these measures is that they are not too difficult to cheat. Tactics for recruiting large numbers of "friends" are well known—there's even software to distribute mass invitations—and numbers of plays can be artificially increased. That's part of the reason the details of Google's calculations of its search results rankings are kept secret, and why Flickr doesn't disclose its process for calculating "interestingness." This secrecy makes it harder to cheat the system, but may also, by the same token, make it harder for creators to trust the system too. The secrecy rules out transparency or independent scrutiny of how the rankings are arrived at; and furthermore, it's far from being a copper-bottomed means of ruling out cheating, since creators who put a premium on getting good rankings can still find ways to boost their showing.

As well as guarding against creators who seek to game or shill the system, intermediaries who produce charts may have to monitor and account for "innocent" biases, such as those introduced when devoted fans seek to exaggerate their listening patterns, as we saw in the last chapter.

You may be wondering if this isn't making too much of a fuss over the charts. Aren't most of them just a bit of harmless fun at the end of the day? Well, if the stakes are high for creators when the chart position influences their placement in playlists, their exposure, and how much attention their work gets, things could get even more serious if these measures influence how much money they receive. This comes back to the declining significance of discrete sales as a means of consuming culture. Digital media is being "bundled" in different ways such that if you buy, say, a subscription to Napster or Last.fm or Netflix, no one can say at the point of purchase how your money should be distributed among the creators whose work is included in the subscription offering. Measuring the relative popularity of different works then becomes critical to how the money is divided.

The prospect of a celestial jukebox where everything is available on demand is the biggest bundle you can imagine. In this scenario, music and other entertainment media flow like water and you pay for the basic service with a flat fee like a utility bill (premium services on top of this may cost extra, just as bottled water does).[134] As the basic service gives you access to just about everything you can think of, the concept of "owning" specific tracks becomes meaningless. Intermediary organizations of some kind would collect the fees and then distribute them to creators based on measures of the popularity of their work. If something like the celestial jukebox scenario comes about, expect some protracted and heated debates about those measures and any exceptions to them.

Spotting and nurturing emerging trends

...**The intermediaries of** the *Net, Blogs and Rock 'n' Roll* era will be more than just police officers and bean counters, however. They will need to nurture emerging creators and active consumers. As well as spotting trends early, they may show leadership in selectively encouraging certain trends—particularly those that reinforce the character of the service they provide.

As intermediaries from the BBC to HMV (a leading UK bricks-and-mortar music retailer) are considering adding social networking to their offerings, it's important to remember that no manager is ever in full control of a social network. You can't treat the behavior of large groups of people as an engineering problem; it's more like gardening or looking after a nature reserve. Just as in a garden things grow and change without you doing anything, so people will discover things in networking sites without any management interventions. However, if parts of the community are left to run wild, that's exactly what they may do.

We saw in Chapter 5 how degrees of intervention differ between intermediaries, from the mostly hands-off approach of Last.fm to the more editor-led model of eMusic. The nature and extent of these interventions affects the character of the online environment, and emphasis on one kind of activity may discourage others. For example, the focus on the editorial and download store features of eMusic may be a factor in making it, in my experience, a less vibrant social space than Last.fm or MySpace: eMusic has a "friends" feature, but it seems to be little used. By contrast, on the MOG music blogging network, the staff often personally welcome new members by commenting on their contributions and befriending them. Apart from that, they blog alongside the members, leading by example and offering support where required.

Social networks that define themselves in terms of their community interaction and word-of-mouth recommendations will want to identify the most active and well-connected members of the network—the Savants, Originators, and other catalysts— who make the community tick. They may also seek to spot any common topics and themes that are regularly cropping up in discussions. Taking a "guide on the side" role, the staff will facilitate connections between members and cross-fertilization of related themes.

To enhance their role as pathways to discovery, these networks and other intermediaries will keep an ear to the ground to identify the up-and-coming creators whose work is starting to generate a buzz. As more creators start to make their names through these new routes, intermediaries are realizing that they can build their own brands through the reputation they gain for "breaking" new artists through to the mainstream, and through the type of artists they break. By their fruits ye shall know them, and the kind of work that first gets an audience through MySpace or Last.fm or LibraryThing (www.librarything.com) influences how consumers perceive these communities.

These up-and-coming artists value the opportunity to develop a strong community of fans under their own steam, without first having to sign up to long-term management and royalty deals. Having already established an audience or a fan base inevitably strengthens their hand when it comes to negotiating deals with labels, studios, publishers, and promoters further down the line. Like an entrepreneur seeking funding for investment, the further you can take your concept toward realizing its potential without outside help, the less control you will have to relinquish when the time comes for you to accept assistance.

Meanwhile, record labels, studios, publishers, and entertainment networks can exploit this DIY economy to reduce the costs of spotting and developing talent. In music, for example, it's a fairly natural progression for an artist to start off in DIY mode, progress to being signed by an independent label, and then move on to the next tier at a major label (either when their contract with the independent expires, or when the independent is bought out by a major).

It's not just new creators who will break through from obscurity to find a larger audience via the new intermediaries. A few artists who have been languishing in the Long Tail for some time, denied the oxygen of visibility by limited retail space and media coverage, may be granted new commercial life and the opportunity to rise up the tail. The Long Tail opens up opportunities for rights owners, too, providing them with a wider range of sources of potential revenue by exploiting their back catalog, though it's unclear as yet how much Long Tail effects can grow the total market, as opposed to redistributing revenue between hits and nonhits.

For social networks and other digital intermediaries to allow works in the Long Tail once again to breathe the oxygen of visibility, they must first recognize them. When I play some of the more obscure tracks in my music collection or enter the ISBN of a rare book, many of the social networks of which I'm a member tell me that they don't recognize the titles concerned. Their catalogs may be extensive, but they have plenty of gaps. And if an item isn't in the catalog, it may not be possible to tag it, include it in a playlist, or start a discussion about it. The coming generation of net services will have to overcome this problem. They will make use of their members, and their members' tastes, to stretch the boundaries of their foraging territory, so that others who share those tastes can make contact with like-minded souls, and still others as yet unfamiliar with such arcane material can make discoveries by following the lead staked out by their peers.

As online intermediaries such as social networks and recommender systems continue to grow in importance as routes to discovery, the managers of these services face considerable challenges in balancing the demands on them. On one hand, the rock 'n' roll ethos of the blog culture that permeates most entertainment-focused online communities is libertarian and promiscuous by nature. On the other, some creators who provide the raw material that inspires these communities will not tolerate people playing fast and loose with their work. Managers have to strike the right balance of regulation that inspires trust from all sides but does not choke the sharing of experiences and discoveries. The new paths to discovery must be inclusive spaces as regards content, creators, and consumers, where anything goes as long as it does not threaten the sustainability of this inclusiveness.

12

Future culture:

Who knows who's next?

Twenty years ago, I came across a couple of experimental filmmakers, Norman McLaren and Bruce Conner, whose work sounded interesting. They are both fairly obscure—though McLaren won many awards, including an Oscar—and I can't remember for sure where I first heard of them. British television showed a short series of Norman McLaren films and something spurred me to tune in. In the case of Bruce Conner, I read a brief profile of him in a copy of *Monthly Film Bulletin*, which I picked up in my local cinema. Conner, I discovered, had made music videos for a couple of bands I liked, and this, together with the rest of the profile, suggested to me that I might like his work. But how could I see it and find out? A program of Conner's short films was touring regional cinemas, but the tour wasn't visiting Sheffield, the city where I lived. On a dark winter evening, I took the 40-minute train journey to Derby and found the cinema where Conner's films were playing for one night only—to a small audience, as it turned out.

I may not be a typical fan, and going to these kinds of lengths isn't typical behavior, even for me. But if you've ever gone out on a limb to discover something, you know the sense of achievement, as well as the buzz of exclusivity, that comes when you stumble on something interesting. If you go to YouTube and search on "Norman McLaren" or "Bruce Conner," you may be able to view a collection of their films.[135] They're short, so it won't take you longer than 15 minutes to view a couple. If you still have a minute to spare, read their profiles on Wikipedia. Having done this, you will have absorbed material similar to that which I gleaned 20 years ago. You may not even have had to leave the room you were sitting in, whereas to see any Conner films I had to wait for the designated Sunday to come around and then journey some distance through the cold. However, when I saw the films I brought to them a focus and an attention (as well as a desire to believe my trip had not been wasted) that I think you will find it hard to match in your YouTube experience.

It's almost a cliché that in a world of on-demand access, if something doesn't take your fancy within a few moments you switch over to something else very quickly. A significant proportion of YouTube's short videos are not watched to the end, and many people skip to the end of songs on their iPods. This points to one of the great paradoxes of the new era of discovery: If everything is always available, why bother to explore it today? It will still be there tomorrow.

One of the things that keeps this pile of entertainment material fresh—and thus holds our interest—is that people keep adding new stuff to it all the time, as well as exhuming old stuff that is remixed or re-evaluated with the "anniversary" treatment. Could there come a point where the pile is so big that we all become jaded and have had enough?

Search Inside the Music

...Paul Lamere leads a project called Search Inside the Music at Sun Microsystems. Sun's interests are in working out how it can support customers for its enormously powerful server computers, which, in the music field, means the capability for catalogs of a mind-boggling number of tracks. The largest databases, at the time of writing, identify tens of millions of tracks. (Apple's iTunes Store and its competitors have catalogs of between two and five million songs.) Paul's job is to think ahead to a world in which these figures increase to hundreds of millions or even billions.

We're talking not just about those tracks that are released by record labels, large and small, but also every track made by teenage dance music enthusiasts in their bedrooms with cheap sequencer software (with each remix counting as a separate track), and every track played by the covers band at your local bar (with each week's version of "Louie, Louie" counting separately). With access to the technology for taking an acoustic "fingerprint" of each track, all amateur musicians could register their work on the global catalog. It would then be available for searching and, subject to licensing, for inclusion in playlists, automated recommendations, and all the other means for helping it find its audience that have been discussed in this book. This is truly the Long Tail.

Lamere conjures up a Holy Grail scenario where your pocket device would be permanently connected to this universe of music. But obviously you don't want to have to navigate through it all to decide what to play next, so the device would have a button that says, "Play me the music that I want to listen to now." It would take into account all the preferences it has picked up in your listening habits, including the proportion of time you spend listening to old favorites compared with new music. It would take account of your current mood and whatever activity you're engaged in. It might harvest the recommendations friends have passed on to you via electronic messages the previous day, slotting them into your playlist next to others with a compatible vibe (and pruning the recommendations from your sister, because she's never sussed what you like, even after you gave her access to your full taste profile).

This is a very ordered version of our cultural future. Like any Holy Grail, it may turn out not to be achievable. How long will it take for competing commercial interests to arrive at a consensus on universal fingerprint identifiers and metadata for audio, video, and other formats? And will the know-how of artificial intelligence and personalization ever get to grips with the contrary nature of our moods and the desires they inspire in us?

Whether it's feasible or not, I'm not sure that the vision of a global entertainment brain from which we all take an individual feed is a desirable one. It feels like an attempt to nail everything down and control it. In other words, it's not rock 'n' roll.

Shake it up

...**Alongside order, we** need something to liven it up, make it *flow*, to disturb and question established perspectives. Many of us with digital music players have turned to shuffle mode, which picks songs from our collections in random order, to stir things up. This is a simple but crude solution. Computers can do artificial intelligence reasonably well, but they can do artificial stupidity—which is what randomness is—pretty much perfectly. It's interesting that this stupidity is such a popular feature. But a richer, more powerful approach is to focus on drawing all this entertainment stuff back into the stream of conversation between people. Animate it by making it part of our evolving relationships. That is, after all, what culture is: the canvas on which we negotiate our shared meanings and identities.

This is where social networks and blogs come into their own. In the Galaxie 500 community that Andy Aldridge initiated (see Chapter 3), individuals with shared interests, but nevertheless prone to differences of opinion, ask each other's views on new bands and albums, using the collective as a research resource, a filter, and a sounding board. On MySpace the social currency of friends and the economic currency of attention are so frequently traded that you could almost set an exchange rate between them. Factors like these influence where we forage in the global database of entertainment, as well as how we interpret what we find there.

Blogs give us an easy medium to express personal opinions publicly, and to animate the global database by drawing our own links between music or films that we see as connected, even if the "authoritative" voices of the mainstream media, like allmusic or Wikipedia, do not. I have said earlier that wikis form part of blog culture, but there is one important respect in which they differ from blogs. The collective, anyone-can-edit nature of wikis means that they efface the individual voices of the contributors. When you read a wiki page (such as a Wikipedia entry), it is difficult to see who has contributed what without forensically and laboriously going through the history of edits to the page. Wikis are such that over time, any outspoken opinions are removed and rough edges are smoothed over. In the case of Wikipedia, a "neutral point of view" is enshrined in editorial policy.[136] By contrast, blogs are all about rough edges. It's usually clear who wrote a blog entry, too, and it's easy to hold that person to account or contradict their opinions by adding a comment to the entry. This means that, taken together, blogs can seem like a chaotic babble, a virtual Tower of Babel. But that characteristic is also what gives them the scope to challenge the status quo, to argue a corner vociferously, and to cajole others round to their way of seeing things.

As outlined in Chapter 9, the coming years will see blogs and social networks used more and more to enhance our experience of events in the real world. This extends from identifying in advance who is going to a club, gig, or cinema screening through to sharing photographs and other recordings afterwards. These are all further means of animating and socializing the cultural experience of the event. Music is unique in this respect, since it exists both as recorded medium and live performance in a way that film, television, games, and writing do not (theater being treated as a distinct art form). The live performance reanimates the recording, helping to make it live and breathe, with the sweat and grit of rock 'n' roll providing a counterfoil to the neat and orderly array of digital catalogs.

Entertaining ourselves to death?

...**Another fear about** the always-available, on-demand world is that it will smooth out our cultural diversity into an undifferentiated mush. Can we kiss goodbye to trends that meant that the center of gravity of popular music kept changing from decade to decade, that children had significantly different tastes from their parents, and that different countries developed diverse traditions? To put these questions into perspective, it's useful to look back at the development of popular culture and technology over the past 50 years or more; indeed, back to the birth of rock 'n' roll.

Around the time Elvis Presley released his first single "That's All Right, Mama," dramatic changes were under way in how people discovered and experienced recorded music. Only time will tell whether the current upheavals in digital entertainment will be seen as more or less significant than that era, but what is clear is that they have a very different character. Whereas the rock 'n' roll era emphasized youth, current trends emphasize what is charitably referred to as "middle youth" (that is, people carrying on their music fan behaviors, once seen as a phase of late adolescence, into their 30s, 40s, and beyond). Rock 'n' roll was perceived as a radical break from the past—a Year Zero of popular culture—but most new music now is keen to emphasize its debt to the traditions of previous generations (including traditions from before the 1950s). As it is now increasingly common for parents and their children to enjoy the same Beatles albums and attend the same Oasis concerts, you could say that, where rock 'n' roll created discord between generations, popular music now brings harmony.

One of the other differences is that in 1954 Elvis's records were seen—by his fans almost as much as by his detractors—as ephemeral objects, subject to the rapid turnover of the hit parade. Now popular music, especially that by Elvis, is a heritage industry, for good or ill. The industries that provide contextual information for popular culture—from magazines, broadcast documentaries, and boxed-set retrospectives to blogs, wikis, and fan communities—have grown phenomenally. Arguably, this is just another way of nailing down the culture, in a move that is against the spirit of rock 'n' roll itself. It certainly offends the traditional rock values of Oasis's Noel Gallagher, who says, in a colorful quote:

> Everyone just wants more and more information. All the fantasy's gone out of music, 'cos everything is too f***ing real. Every album comes with a DVD with some c*** going, "Yeah well, we tried the drums over there, but..." Give a shit, man! It makes people seem too human, whereas I was brought up on Marc Bolan and David Bowie, and it was like, "Do they actually come from f***ing Mars?"[137]

How have the differences between now and the 1950s come about? There is no single answer. Technology played a part, but so did demographic, economic, social, and cultural trends.

Record sales jumped fivefold between 1945 and 1958.[138] Many factors contributed to this explosive growth. Electric guitars and amplification reached the mass market; the Gibson Les Paul and the Fender Stratocaster (still the two most iconic models of electric guitar) were both introduced in the early 1950s. In 1948 Columbia Records introduced the 33⅓ rpm long playing record, and the following year RCA responded with the 45 rpm single. In those days it was the record labels that instigated and owned the format innovations, not independent technology providers. But radio, the primary means of discovering music, was managed independently from the record industry, and it was the spread of cheap transistor radios that brought this discovery within the range of the young. The portability of these devices took them out of the living room and beyond parental control. In his book *Playback*, Mark Coleman argues that it was catchy 45 rpm singles together with transistor radios that helped give birth to rock 'n' roll.

By the end of the 1950s, the first baby boomers were becoming teenagers and, in contrast to a previous generation that had grown up in times of economic depression followed by wartime austerity, they had enough money to buy singles and radios for themselves. In the UK, postwar rationing did not end until the middle of that decade, and it was natural that the culture of the period should recognize this watershed with increased exuberance and self-confidence, though these were laced with anomie by the emerging generation, giving rise to Angry Young Men and *Rebel Without a Cause*.

Half a century on, global music sales are falling, despite digital growth, while DVD sales and cinema admissions have reached a plateau. Large volumes of illicit file sharing indicate that appetites are still strong. However, many observers believe that the rate of change in music culture itself has slowed to a crawl. Consider, for example, this observation from the critic John Harris, writing in *The Guardian* in 2006:

> Older readers will attest to the fact that 1977 was
> very unlike 1967: in the intervening years—and
> this is somewhat crude, but bear with me—

psychedelia turned to prog, which was in turn avenged by punk, while glam-rock strutted about and the music industry inaugurated the age of the singer-songwriter. This year, by contrast, isn't that different from 1996: Blur and the Gallaghers are still here, the cranked-up guitar remains king, and it's still just about acceptable to walk around with a Britpop haircut (I should know—I've got one).[139]

The factors that have contributed to the musical landscape becoming becalmed are as varied as those that whipped it into a frenzy 50 years ago. To pick a handful of examples, first, the new technology of choice for today's music makers is sampling. Where electric guitars in the 1950s and the first synthesizers in the 1960s made new and alien sounds (almost literally in the synthesizers' case), sampling and its application in musical mash-ups emphasize continuity and tradition. Notwithstanding the treatments that can be applied to samples, sampling produces sounds that have all been heard before. In addition, demographically almost all western societies are ageing, and teenagers inhabit a world that is culturally and economically not that different from the one their parents grew up in, except that there is more of everything to choose from. Older generations have seen new musical "rebellions" come and go and, rather than demonize them as folk devils and moral panics, they accept them with a sanguine shrug. Sometimes, as when the Nobel prize winner for literature Seamus Heaney praised Eminem's verbal energy,[140] high culture openly acknowledges the vitality of new music instead of just moralizing about its profanity.

So even rock 'n' roll doesn't seem very rock 'n' roll any more. The emphasis on tradition in rock, pop, and dance music means they have almost turned into what they originally threatened to overthrow: folk music. Not folk music as in accordions and pipe smoking, but folk music as a set of vernacular traditions that interweave with each other, reviving, covering, sampling, and stealing musical ideas, buffing them up and re-presenting them in alternative contexts and arrangements. Sounds like the definition of a digital mash-up, doesn't it?

It's not just sampling that encourages this propensity to confine listening within established traditions. The technologies to support discovery that this book has described are so powerful and so efficient that they make it easy to be a lazy and unadventurous forager. If you try out something new and it doesn't take your fancy within 30 seconds, Google, iTunes, or MySpace can find you something else to try out in the blink of an eye. The downside of this convenience is that the music or video that is genuinely original, and doesn't easily fit within existing genres and pigeonholes, often will not reveal its qualities without extended listening and repeated trying out. That which references the past, on the other hand, is quicker to appeal and easier to digest. And even serious Savants, offered the scope of unlimited, all-you-can-eat music subscription services, have been heard to grumble, "I'm so busy downloading stuff to listen to when and where I want that I've run out of time to listen to it."

Thus Joe Boyd, a 60-something music producer and manager who built his career first by finding an audience for the jazz and blues performers he discovered in his youth, and then by supporting the careers of a new generation of folk-rock artists, sounds a pessimistic note when he writes:

> History today seems more like a postmodern collage; we are surrounded by two-dimensional representations of our heritage. Access via amazon.com or iPod to all those boxed sets of old blues singers—or Nick Drake, for that matter—doesn't equate with the sense of discovery and connection [my generation] experienced. The very

existence of such a wealth of information creates
an overload that can drown out vivid moments of
revelation.[141]

If we want to depress ourselves, we can run this scenario
forward and make an analogy with the laws of thermodynamics
in the universe, which say that, ultimately, all the stars will burn
out and, instead of hot and cold, everything will be lukewarm
and grey. When the Long Tail effect makes itself felt, the
distribution of attention and sales will be evened out, so that hits
won't be such big hits, and misses won't be such flops. Will
more of our cultural experiences occupy a safe, neutral middle
ground?

It's up to us

    ...I don't think we're heading for cultural meltdown
or the end of history. Everyone from millenarian cults to
professors of political economy has predicted this at some time
or other, but whenever you think history or culture is grinding to
a halt before your eyes, it pops up energetically in exactly the
spot where you weren't looking and bites your behind.
    The Long Tail is an aggregate of millions of people's
activity, not a template for each of us individually. That means
that it can shelter a lot of diversity and eccentricity under its
curve without losing its trademark shape. Indeed, the extra
length of the tail is a measure of increased diversity.
    I am sympathetic to the it-ain't-what-it-used-to-be
laments of Gallagher, Harris, and Boyd. The losses they mark—of
mystery, the rapid turnover of ideas, and vivid moments of
revelation—should not be taken lightly. However, to point out that
there are diseases or curses of affluence is not to say that affluence
is undesirable. This affluence is the on-demand, information-

saturated access to a massive catalog of entertainment and culture. Surely no previous generation would have rejected this opportunity, had they had it within their grasp; and it is our responsibility to fulfill its potential.

How do we discharge this responsibility? We need systems that help us forage for and identify mysterious, innovative, and vivid cultural experiences, while acknowledging (following on from the quotes from William Goldman and Richard Feynman cited earlier in the book) that no one really knows how to do this. When it comes to methods for discovery, anything goes. We need to tap the wisdom of crowds, but to guard against herd instinct and mob rule. We need effective measures recognizing that any participative medium that affects the attention and revenue artists receive is going to attract attempts to bias and distort it, and that these attempts need to be foiled. Above all, we need methods and technologies that are people centric as much as, if not more than, information centric.

Can we expect Apple, Amazon, Google, MySpace, or the BBC to provide this? It depends how they seek to exert control. I described in Chapter 9 how the Web 2.0 approach puts a focus on innovation rather than efficiency, with modular systems that let solutions emerge organically rather than engineering them in advance. In different ways, these corporations are experimenting with handing over some control to their users, customers, and audiences. MySpace, for example, doesn't take responsibility for producing any of the main content on its site.

Corporations that seek to control developments in the era of digital discovery rely on predictability; and predictability is in short supply. You can make things more predictable by hedging and going for safe bets, like supporting the film studios, record labels, and artists who were successful *last* year. But then you miss the cutting edge. And ultimately, all large corporations desire some degree of control and predictability, because they are important ingredients for the sustained viability of their enterprises.

Perhaps the alternative, then, is for the technology and media providers to hand over the means of discovery to us, the social proletariat of the networking age. Recently a strategy adviser to the UK government spoke of the impact of the net as creating an electorate "unwilling to be governed but not yet capable of self-government."[142] Of course he was castigated by citizen groups for this opinion, but could there be an element of truth in what he said? It is still very early days in the evolution of what is called "user-generated content," the umbrella term for blogs, wikis, comments, discussion boards, and audience ratings.

Wikipedia is, so far, one of the great successes in the field. Its model aggregates modest volunteer effort from many of us according to our expertise, and then makes it available to everyone according to their demand. If this can be sustained and extended, it will truly be one of the landmark achievements of our age. But it will by no means be sufficient on its own. Alongside such aggregated, collective productions, we also need strong individual voices to articulate new perspectives and challenge the status quo. This is where we depend on our Savants (Chapter 2) and Originators (Chapter 3), and their blogs, to form the vanguard of taste and set the pace of innovation.

Will we get what we need? No one can offer any guarantees. But the lesson of history is that if cheap tools are available, from electric guitars and transistor radios through personal computers to blogs and wikis, interesting stuff will emerge from somewhere. The established order may not like it at first, but in time they will adapt to it and even incorporate it.

From what direction is this interesting stuff coming, and how will we recognize it when we see it? Who knows? It quite possibly won't look like what we're used to—the first of Malcolm Gladwell's three rules of "cool" is that the act of discovering *cool* causes *cool* to move on.[143]

As I've said, my instinct is that the motor of history is not running out of juice; but the juice has to come from somewhere. In the terminology of electricity, an electrical current flows whenever there is a difference in potential between two points. Differences in potential arise all around us, locally and globally. Fifty years ago there was a generation gap that fueled the birth of rock 'n' roll. Then there was the culture gap between the US and UK that led to The Beatles and the Rolling Stones discovering the blues of the American South before mainstream America did, and re-importing it back to the States as the "British invasion." Where are the new gaps that will energize the next wave of change?

On the net, there will be a growing difference between the Anglophone online culture and that which grows in India and China, for example. Differences between national cultures are beyond the scope of this book, but it is already apparent that some countries have taken to blogging very rapidly (France being a notable example) while others are lagging behind. If there are differences in the dynamics of online word of mouth between different places, it may be that new discoveries diffuse at different rates or in different ways.

The new generation of so-called "digital natives" includes everyone now entering adulthood, who has grown up with access to the net and all its communication potential without ever knowing anything different. The digital natives, it is said, are impatient with any content or media that doesn't provide them with the means to blog it, remix it, and share it. Will this generation turn our media upside-down? It remains to be seen, for example, whether the proportion of people who create or edit Wikipedia entries, as opposed just to reading them, will increase significantly from its current tiny percentage. So there may be a new generation gap; but even within generations there will continue to be a gap between Savants and Casuals, between Originators and Lurkers, between the cool people and the rest of us.

As the means of creating digital audio and video continue to get cheaper, and independent creative production becomes possible for a wider group of people, the gap between the independent sector and the major entertainment empires doesn't look like getting any narrower (though there may be more artists and companies occupying the middle ground between the extremes). The independent sector has historically been more willing to take risks and try out new methods. Many will fail to make a living out of enterprises in the Long Tail, but some will succeed, and a few will break out of the "tail" altogether and challenge the big guys with new hits. We should expect the unexpected, including some paradoxes, such as the underground networks of bands and distributors who maintain their exclusive cool status by being digital refuseniks. They produce vinyl records rather than downloads and sell them at low-key gigs and via hobbyist web stores that despatch orders from the kitchen table.

We can't be sure whether future generations will see the present era as revolution or evolution. However, the most rapid and significant changes will come about with the alignment of many factors. These include lower barriers to issuing recordings, better ways of rating entertainment and spotting winners, tapping the energy of amateur fans, the willingness of the independent sector to try out new ideas, and improved relationships between artists, producers, and consumers. By mixing this rich stew of ingredients according to the *Net, Blogs and Rock 'n' Roll* recipe, we can surely cook up something that both stimulates and satisfies.

Acknowledgments...

First and foremost I'd like to thank Lucy Vickery, whose love, support, and contributions helped see me through every stage of writing this book. Seb Schmoller and Paul Lamere went beyond just giving comments and were also a regular source of encouragement and ideas. Thanks also to Annie Weekes for her detailed assessment of my draft, and many useful suggestions.

Many people gave their time to speak to me as I put the book together. The contributions of Andy Aldridge, Martin Stiksel, Paul Lamere, Matthew Shorter, Dan Hill, and Zac Johnson are mentioned in the text, but thanks are also due to Frances Maxwell, Anthony Volodkin of The Hype Machine, and James Walton. Eric Namour of [no.signal] advised me on scenarios for event promoters that unfortunately had to be cut from this version. Mark Clark, Colin Donald, Jan Ellis, and Kate Theophilus were interested in what I was writing about and swapped ideas. John Buckman of Magnatune, Gerd Leonhard of Sonific, and Adrian North of the University of Leicester gave me very prompt comments on what I'd written about them. Michael Bull sent me his latest research with iPod users. Elizabeth Wells and Gabriel Aldamiz-echevarria of MyStrands gave me permission, at short notice, to reproduce Figure 2 in the text, and I'm grateful too to MyStrands for inviting me to the excellent Recommenders '06 Summer School in Bilbao, Spain (disclosure in keeping with blog culture: I paid all my expenses, but definitely owe them a few beers).

My old friend Jeremy Thwaites brainstormed title ideas. "The vibe-raters" is him all over. Nicola Winter and Katherine Davey advised me on the original book proposal.

This is my first proper book and shepherding someone like me through a first book, including disabusing me of my misconceptions, is not a task I envy. Thanks to Nicholas Brealey and Sally Lansdell for sticking with it.

Most of the writing was a solitary activity, and everyone needs a bit of distraction. A tip of the hat, then, to all involved with the Gideon Coe show on BBC 6 Music for their high-quality distractions (plus one useful contribution: I discovered gothicsouls.com, mentioned in the book, via the show's "Website Wasteland" feature).

Notes

Several of the notes include addresses of web pages where you can consult my sources directly. Unless otherwise noted, these addresses have been checked and were current as of 6 January 2007. More direct links and resources are available via www.netblogsrocknroll.com.

1   www.iamplify.com, http://tapeitofftheinternet.com, http://eventful.com, http://upcoming.org, www.fictionwise.com, and http://realtravel.com.
2   Chris Anderson (2006) *The Long Tail: How Endless Choice Is Creating Unlimited Demand*, Random House.
3   www.jamendo.com and http://amiestreet.com.
4   One of the initial presentations of this theory can be found in Pirolli, P. & Card, S. K. (1999) "Information foraging," *Psychological Review*, 106(4): 643–75. This and other papers by Peter Pirolli about the theory can be found at www2.parc.com/istl/groups/uir/publications/author/Pirolli_ab.html. The references to foraging throughout this book do not follow closely the information foraging theory developed by Pirolli and colleagues, which include sophisticated mathematical models for predicting behavior. In the main I have just adopted the metaphors at the heart of the theory.
5   "Information foraging: Why Google makes people leave your site faster," *Jakob Nielsen's Alertbox*, 30 June 2003, www.useit.com/alertbox/20030630.html.
6   "Novice vs. expert users," *Jakob Nielsen's Alertbox*, 6 February 2000, www.useit.com/alertbox/20000206.html.
7   Paul Morley (2003) *Words and Music*, Bloomsbury.
8   "David Goldberg on Yahoo's value in music," *Billboard PostPlay*, 2 March 2005, http://billboard.blogs.com/billboardpostplay/2005/03/david_goldberg_.html.
9   Markus Giesler (2006) "Consumer gift system: Netnographic insights from Napster," *Journal of Consumer Research*, September: 283–90. Also available via www.markus-giesler.de/publications.htm.
10 These figures are taken from two BBC News stories: "Lost records 'fuel digital drive,'" *BBC News Online*, 15 November 2005, http://news.bbc.co.uk/1/hi/entertainment/music/4436414.stm; and "Music collections 'worth £1,500,'" *BBC News Online*, 17 June 2005, http://news.bbc.co.uk/1/hi/entertainment/music/4102786.stm (which in turn is based on a poll by research company ICM, reported at http://tinyurl.com/dnoya). Note that the higher figure (178) is based on data from men only.
11 "Music buyers 'are growing older,'" *BBC News Online*, 2 August 2005,

http://news.bbc.co.uk/1/hi/entertainment/music/4738181.stm, based on figures from the International Federation of the Phonographic Industry.

12   "Age no bar as baby boomers rock the music industry," *The Guardian*, 28 November 2006, http://music.guardian.co.uk/news/story/0,,1958516,00.html.

13   "Melody maker," *The Guardian*, 1 March 2004, www.guardian.co.uk/ arts/features/story/0,11710,1159112,00.html. There has been a trend over recent years for the proportion of album sales to younger age groups to decline while the proportion of sales to older groups increases. In 2002, the 12–19 age group accounted for 16.4% of album sales, the 40–49 age group for 19.1%, and the 50–59 age group for 14.3%. The people who became music Savants and Enthusiasts from the 1960s onwards appear to have staying power.

14   Evan Eisenberg (2005) *The Recording Angel: Music, Records and Culture from Aristotle to Zappa*, 2nd edn, Yale University Press.

15   At the time of the research Emap had four music magazines, but it closed its largest pop title *Smash Hits* early in 2006 due to falling circulation. The circulation of its heritage and specialist magazines *Mojo*, *Q*, and *Kerrang!* has been rising.

16   Details and downloads of the Project Phoenix research were published at www.emapadvertising.com/insight/project_detail.asp?CaseStudyID=136. Project Phoenix 2 materials are at www.emapadvertising.com/insight/ project_detail.asp?CaseStudyID=163.

17   "Upbeat about downloading? You could be out of pocket," *The Observer*, 1 May 2005, http://observer.guardian.co.uk/cash/story/0,,1473919,00.html.

18   IFPI Digital Music Reports 2005 and 2007, www.ifpi.org/content/ section_news/20050119.html and www.ifpi.org/content/section_resources/ digital-music-report.html (accessed 29 January 2007).

19   Since 2003 when the research was conducted the average price of both CDs and broadband has declined. ("Quid" is English slang for a pound sterling.)

20   The book that defined this area was probably Dick Hebdige (1979) *Subculture: The Meaning of Style*, Routledge.

21   Raymond MacDonald, Dorothy Miell, & Graeme Wilson (2005) "Talking about music: A vehicle for identity development," in Dorothy Miell, Raymond MacDonald, and David J. Hargreaves (eds), *Musical Communication*, Oxford University Press.

22   Malcolm Gladwell (2000) *The Tipping Point: How Little Things Can Make a Big Difference*, Abacus. Wikipedia has a concise overview of the book's concepts, including Connectors, Mavens, and Salesmen, at http:// en.wikipedia.org/wiki/The_Tipping_Point_(book).

23   These terms are taken from pages 8 and 107 of Justin Kirby & Paul Marsden (eds) (2006) *Connected Marketing: The Viral, Buzz and Word of Mouth Revolution*, Butterworth-Heinemann.

24   Sven Rusticus, "Creating brand advocates," in Kirby & Marsden, *op. cit.*

25   Bradley Horowitz (2006) "Creators, synthesizers, and consumers," *Elatable*, 17 February, www.elatable.com/blog/?p=5. Horowitz's figures appear to be based only on data from Yahoo! Groups, but are backed up by a range of data

from other sources, reported by web usability expert Jakob Nielsen, who refers to the issue as "participation inequality" ("Participation inequality: Encouraging more users to contribute," *Alertbox*, 9 October 2006, www.useit.com/alertbox/ participation_inequality.html).

26   Donald Clark (2006) "Everyone writes and no one pays," March, http://fm.schmoller.net/2006/03/everyone_writes.html.

27   http://en.wikipedia.org/wiki/Wikipedia provides as a measure the 27,000 users who made at least five edits, and 4,000 users who made 100 or more edits during the month of December 2005, while http://en.wikipedia.org/w/index.php?title=Wikipedia:Wikipedians&oldid=33575412 gives the number of registered users at that time as over 700,000 (supplemented by an "unknown but quite large" number of unregistered contributors).

28   This pattern is described at greater length in Aaron Swartz (2006), "Who writes Wikipedia?," www.aaronsw.com/weblog/whowriteswikipedia.

29   www.cityofsound.com/blog/2006/03/why_lost_is_gen.html. Hill also notes Steven Johnson's term "para-sites" to refer to the same phenomenon.

30   For more extended discussion on Second Life and related developments, see J. D. Lasica (2005) *Darknet: Hollywood's War Against the Digital Generation*, John Wiley; or Don Tapscott & Anthony D. Williams (2006) *Wikinomics: How Mass Collaboration Changes Everything*, Portfolio.

31   The key text in this area is Etienne Wenger (1998) *Communities of Practice: Learning, Meaning, and Identity*, Cambridge University Press. There is a brief introduction to the concepts at www.ewenger.com/theory.

32   As often occurs between artists and dedicated fan communities, a finely nuanced discourse of ethics arises around issues like amateur not-for-profit bootleg recordings of live gigs. Fans and artists may feel that these recordings pose no threat to sales of professional studio recordings, and artists may take a stance of neither moving to prevent it or (explicitly) condoning it. The lines between what is and is not acceptable practice are drawn differently for different artists, and their precise location is something that novice community members will pick up informally from the old hands.

33   Etienne Wenger (undated) "Communities of practice: A brief introduction," www.ewenger.com/theory.

34   Lee Rainie (2007) "28% of online Americans have used the Internet to tag content," Pew Internet and American Life Project, www.pewinternet.org/PPF/r/201/report_display.asp (accessed 4 February 2007).

35   Dylan Jones (2005) *iPod Therefore I Am: A Personal Journey through Music*, Weidenfeld and Nicholson.

36   The fictional celebrity playlist is a form I have explored myself, creating playlists that could have been compiled by Neil Young, Philip Jeays, and others. These playlists are linked from the book site at www.netblogsrocknroll.com.

37   Amy Voida, Rebecca E. Grinter, Nicolas Ducheneaut, W. Keith Edwards, & Mark W. Newman (2005) "Listening in: Practices surrounding iTunes music sharing," *Proceedings of the CHI 2005 Conference*, ACM. At the time of the research, the iTunes software allowed users on the same subnet of a local area

network to share music between their computers.

38   Erving Goffman (1959) *The Presentation of Self in Everyday Life*, Doubleday.

39   www.mystrands.com/top (accessed 19 October 2006).

40   www.last.fm/charts/music/artist (accessed 19 October 2006).

41   Matthew J. Salganik, Peter Sheridan Dodds, & Duncan J. Watts (2006) "Experimental study of inequality and unpredictability in an artificial cultural market," *Science*, 311(5762): 854–56, www.sciencemag.org/cgi/content/abstract/311/5762/854.

42   Quoted from Platinum Blue website home page, www.platinumblueinc.com (accessed 18 October 2006). For more on this technology, see "Making hit music into a science," *BBC News*, 15 June 2006, http://news.bbc.co.uk/1/hi/entertainment/5083986.stm.

43   See, for example, the story of 2bigfeet.com in John Battelle (2005) *The Search: How Google and its Rivals Rewrote the Rules of Business and Transformed our Culture*, Nicholas Brealey Publishing.

44   James Surowiecki (2004) *The Wisdom of Crowds*, Doubleday.

45   "Classical music makes digital leap," *Reuters*, 21 January 2006, http://tinyurl.com/9g2jd (accessed 23 January 2006).

46   "Big demand for classical downloads is music to ears of record industry," *The Guardian*, 28 March 2006, http://arts.guardian.co.uk/netmusic/story/0,,1741087,00.html.

47   http://en.wikipedia.org/wiki/UK_classical_chart (accessed 6 January 2006).

48   Louis Barfe (2004) *Where Have All the Good Times Gone?*, Atlantic Books.

49   In September 2006, MySpace said it hosted over 3 million recording artists ("MySpace to let members sell music," *Wired News*, www.wired.com/news/wireservice/0,71713-0.html). In November 2006, the iTunes Store claimed over 3.5 million songs (www.apple.com/itunes/store, accessed 25 November 2006).

50   C. Marlow, M. Naaman, d. boyd, & M. Davis (2006) "Position paper, tagging, taxonomy, Flickr, article, ToRead," paper presented to WWW2006 Tagging Workshop, available via www.rawsugar.com/www2006/29.pdf.

51   Andrew Keen (2007) *The Cult of the Amateur: How Today's Internet Is Killing our Culture and Assaulting our Economy*, Nicholas Brealey.

52   "The politics of the playful web," *Test* (Matt Locke's blog), 3 March 2005, www.test.org.uk/archives/002380.html.

53   The edited article, "Veni, vidi, Wiki," can be found at www.wired.com/news/technology/0,71733-0.html and Singel's commentary is at www.wired.com/news/technology/0,71737-0.html.

54   "Bob Dylan record sales go through the roof," *NME*, 1 October 2005, www.nme.com/news/bob-dylan/21130.

55   The archive of "Readers Recommend" playlist features can be found at http://music.guardian.co.uk/readersrecommend/0,,1929388,00.html.

56   Chris Anderson (2004) "The Long Tail," *Wired*, October, www.wired.com/wired/archive/12.10/tail.html.

57   My account of the Global Jukebox is based largely on the writings of Michael Naimark, who was part of the project team with Alan Lomax. These writings

can be found at www.naimark.net/projects/jukebox.html. Martin Edlund also describes his interaction with the Global Jukebox prototype in his article "The Madonna Code: Searching for the perfect music recommendation system," *Slate*, 5 July 2005, www.slate.com/id/2121998.

58   This account is based on Gage Averill (2003) "Cantometrics and cultural equity: The academic years," in Ronald D. Cohen (ed.), *Alan Lomax: Selected Writings 1934–1997*, Routledge.

59   Pandora FAQ at http://blog.pandora.com/faq (accessed 8 February 2007).

60   See, for example, David Porter, "How best to discover," 25 January 2006, http://davidporter.wordpress.com/2006/01/25/6; Steve Krause, "Pandora and Last.fm: Nature vs nurture in music recommenders," 30 January 2006, www.stevekrause.org/steve_krause_blog/2006/01/pandora_and_las.html; Chris Dahlen, "Better than we know ourselves," *Pitchfork*, 22 May 2006, http://pitchforkmedia.com/article/feature/36524/Better_Than_We_Know_Ourselves.

61   A much more extensive list of attributes appeared on Wikipedia at http://en.wikipedia.org/wiki/List_of_Music_Genome_Project_attributes.

62   "Outside the box—Pandora rekindles the magic of music," *Star News Online*, http://tinyurl.com/n9wov.

63   Pandora FAQ at http://blog.pandora.com/faq (accessed 8 February 2007).

64   Ian Cross (2005) "Music and meaning, ambiguity and evolution," in Miell, MacDonald, & Hargreaves, *op. cit.*, p. 30.

65   Brian Eno (1994) "Resonant complexity," *Whole Earth Review*, Summer 1994. An excerpt is available via http://music.hyperreal.org/artists/brian_eno/resonant.html.

66   Peter Wollen (1976) "*North by Northwest*: A morphological analysis," *Film Form*, 1: 19–34. Wikipedia has a good basic introduction to Propp's framework at http://en.wikipedia.org/wiki/Vladimir_Propp.

67   Quotes in the text are taken from A. C. North, D. J. Hargreaves, & J. J. Hargreaves (2004) "The uses of music in everyday life," *Music Perception*, 22: 63–99. Media coverage includes: "Download generation 'apathetic,'" *BBC News*, 10 January 2006, http://news.bbc.co.uk/1/hi/entertainment/4599340.stm; "Downloads in music overload," *Scotland on Sunday*, 11 December 2005, http://news.scotsman.com/scitech.cfm?id=2384402005.

68   www.apple.com/ipod/nike.

69   The best-known commentary is Walter Benjamin's essay "The work of art in the age of mechanical reproduction," included in the *Illuminations* collection of his writings (Schocken Books, 1968).

70   Brian Eno (1996) "Ambient music," in *A Year with Swollen Appendices*, Faber and Faber.

71   Mark Coleman (2004) *Playback: From the Victrola to MP3, 100 Years of Music, Machines, and Money*, Da Capo Press.

72   Michael Bull (2000) *Sounding Out the City: Personal Stereos and the Management of Everyday Life*, Berg. Michael Bull has a new book, *Sound Moves: iPod Culture and Urban Experience*, due to be published by Routledge in 2007.

73   Michael Bull (2005) "No dead air! The iPod and the culture of mobile listening," *Leisure Studies*, 24(October): 343–55. See also "Bull session with Professor iPod," *Wired News*, 24 February 2004, www.wired.com/news/mac/0,2125,62396,00.html.

74   Marcia J. Bates (2002) "Toward an integrated model of information seeking and searching," Keynote paper for The Fourth International Conference on Information Needs, Seeking and Use in Different Contexts, Lisbon, available via www.gseis.ucla.edu/faculty/bates/articles/info_SeekSearch-i-030329.html.

75   Battelle, *op. cit.*

76   For an analysis of how iTunes diminishes the resources for discovery compared with vinyl record covers, see Wayne Bremser (2004) "iTunes versus Preservation," www.harlem.org/itunes/index.html.

77   The de facto standard for metadata in MP3 files is called ID3 tags. This standard has gone through various versions, though the latest version has only slowly gained widespread acceptance and use.

78   David Weinberger (2002) *Small Pieces Loosely Joined: How the Web Shows Us Who We Really Are*, Perseus Press, p. 141.

79   John Seely Brown & Paul Duguid (2000) *The Social Life of Information*, Harvard Business School Press.

80   del.icio.us can be found at http://del.ico.us and Furl is at www.furl.net.

81   The exact figures vary in different tellings of this story. These are taken from Sandi Thom's website, www.sandithom.com/site/sandi.php.

82   "Music groups in detail," Project Phoenix research download, www.emapadvertising.com/insight/project_detail.asp?CaseStudyID=136.

83   "eMusic checks into Westin Hotels deal," *Billboard.Biz*, 4 May 2006, http://tinyurl.com/vnbor.

84   David Kusek & Gerd Leonhard (2005) *The Future of Music: Manifesto for the Digital Music Revolution*, Berklee Press.

85   Personal email to the author.

86   Andrew Corcoran, Paul Marsden, Thomas Zorbach, & Bernd Röthlingshöfer, "Blog Marketing," in Kirby & Marsden, *op. cit.*

87   "Message forum spam," *MetaFilter Community Weblog*, 25 January 2005, www.metafilter.com/mefi/38963. See also "Web of Lies," *.net magazine*, May 2005, www.netmag.co.uk/features/default.asp?pagetypeid=2&articleid=36238.

88   www.jose-gonzalez.com (accessed 28 November 2006).

89   Both sides of this story are explored in "An internet superstar—or just another rock'n'roll swindle?," *The Guardian*, 31 May 2006, http://arts.guardian.co.uk/netmusic/story/0,,1786403,00.html. A detailed chronology of key points in Sandi Thom's rise, and some of the controversy surrounding them, is recorded at http://en.wikipedia.org/wiki/Sandi_Thom.

90   Quoted in "Web of lies," *.net magazine*, May 2005, www.netmag.co.uk.

91   See, for example, "BurnLounge—Still ripping off consumers?," *Digital Music Weblog*, http://digitalmusic.weblogsinc.com/2006/07/19/burnlounge-still-ripping-consumers-off, and "BurnLounge—MLM comes to digital music," *Digital Music News*, www.digitalmusicnews.com/blog/310.

92   "MySpace to let members sell music," *Wired News*, 2 September 2006,

www.wired.com/news/wireservice/0,71713-0.html.

93   Through services like Nielsen BuzzMetrics' Blogpulse (www.blogpulse.com).

94   Kirby & Marsden, *op. cit.*, p. xxvi.

95   "Weird web trail: Conspiracy theory—or marketing for Nine Inch Nails LP?,"
      MTV News, 15 February 2007, www.mtv.com/news/articles/1552470/
      20070215/nine_inch_nails.jhtml (accessed 22 March 2007).

96   "The real secret of Blair Witch," *Fortune*, 18 September 2000,
      http://money.cnn.com/magazines/fortune/fortune_archive/2000/09/18/287666.

97   "The taste-makers," *The Guardian*, 30 September 2005, http://
      arts.guardian.co.uk/filmandmusic/story/0,,1580828,00.html.

98   When the single came out in the US, Amazon.com's editorial review reported,
      slightly curiously, that it had "gate crashed the UK charts at #1 and no-one
      saw it coming... except the fans!" But as film-maker John Ford said, "When
      the legend becomes fact, print the legend."

99   John Seely Brown & John Hagel III (2005) "From push to pull: The next frontier
      of innovation," *The McKinsey Quarterly*, 3, www.mckinseyquarterly.com/
      links/18708.

100   William Goldman (1996) *Adventures in the Screen Trade: A Personal View of
      Hollywood*, Abacus.

101   In 2004, Robin Sloan and Matt Thompson created a short flash animation that
      purported to have been made in 2014. It described a scenario where Google
      and Amazon had merged to create Googlezon, to combine the data storage
      and indexing of the former with the collaborative filtering and
      recommendations of the latter. For more details see http://en.wikipedia.org/
      wiki/Googlezon.

102   The services described in this paragraph are, at the time of writing, not part of
      the mainstream MyStrands service, but are in the development labs section of
      its site at http://labs.mystrands.com/features/recommendations/lastfmrecs.html.

103   See, for example, Leon Benjamin (2005) *Winning by Sharing: A New Way of
      Working, a Different Way of Doing Business*, Business for Good.

104   Robert Scoble & Shel Israel (2006) *Naked Conversations: How Blogs are
      Changing the Way Businesses Talk with Customers*, John Wiley.

105   *The School of Rock* (2003), written by Mike White, Paramount Pictures. Full
      quote www.imdb.com/title/tt0332379/quotes.

106   For an analysis of the social currency and dynamics of hanging out, see danah
      boyd (2006) "Identity production in a networked culture: Why youth heart
      MySpace," transcript of talk given to American Association for the
      Advancement of Science, available via www.danah.org/papers/AAAS2006.
      html.

107   Clay Shirky wrote "Social software is stuff that gets spammed" on his blog at
      http://many.corante.com/archives/2005/02/01/tags_run_amok.php.

108   For example, I recommend both the book and accompanying CD for Joe Boyd
      (2006) *White Bicycles: Making Music in the 1960s*, Serpents Tail; and Sean
      Wilentz & Greil Marcus's (2004) collection *The Rose and the Briar: Death,
      Love and Liberty in the American Ballad*, W. W. Norton.

109   This paragraph is based on Tom Coates, "On the BBC Annotatable Audio

project...," *plasticbag.org* blog, 28 October 2005, www.plasticbag.org/archives/2005/10/on_the_bbc_annotatable_audio_project/. At the time of writing, the BBC is piloting this service as "Find, Listen, Label."

110 Owen Myers' Lyricator software can be found at http://web.media.mit.edu/~meyers/lyricator.html. It analyzes a song's lyrics on three dimensions (pleasure/displeasure, arousal/nonarousal, and dominance/submissiveness), and then classifies the mood of the song based on its position in these dimensions.

111 See, for example, "Grouper just says "no" to Kenny G," *TechCrunch*, 6 January 2007, www.techcrunch.com/2007/01/06/grouper-just-says-no-to-kenny-g.

112 "Record company suspends kids' PR scheme," *The Guardian*, 21 December 2004, http://media.guardian.co.uk/marketingandpr/story/0,,1377667,00.html.

113 The ideas in this paragraph owe a lot to a talk given by John Riedl at the Recommenders '06 summer school in Bilbao, Spain. Details of this talk can be found at http://blog.recommenders06.com/?p=12.

114 "Record bought at flea market fetches $155,401," CNN.com, 10 December 2006, www.cnn.com/2006/SHOWBIZ/Music/12/10/vintage.velvet.ap/index.html. The winning bid later turned out to be a fraud, but it seems unlikely that all the high bids were insincere.

115 Henry Jenkins, "I want my Geek TV!," *Flow*, 1(3), September 2005, http://jot.communication.utexas.edu/flow/?jot=view&id=936.

116 "Web 2.0 – Google CEO – Take Your Data and Run," *Network World*, 7 November 2006, www.networkworld.com/news/2006/110806-web-20-google-ceo-take.html.

117 See, for example, AttentionTrust (www.attentiontrust.org) and Attention Profiling Mark-up Language (www.apml.org).

118 For more on this case, see "Privacy fears shock Facebook," *Wired News*, 7 September 2006, www.wired.com/news/technology/0,71739-0.html. For more detail, see danah boyd, "Facebook's 'privacy trainwreck": Exposure, invasion, and drama," *Apophenia Blog*, 8 September 2006, www.danah.org/papers/FacebookAndPrivacy.html; and Fred Stutzman, "Case study: Facebook feeds and networked political action," *Unit Structures* blog, 2006, http://chimprawk.blogspot.com/2006/11/case-study-facebook-feeds-and.html.

119 "Snooping fears plague new iTunes," *BBC News*, 13 January 2006, http://news.bbc.co.uk/1/hi/technology/4608882.stm.

120 Andrew Carton's *Treonauts* blog (http://blogs.treonauts.com) is one of the best-known examples.

121 In a typical display of transparency, Andy publishes the revenue he earns from the site (see www.grange85.co.uk/galaxie/index.php?article_id=159).

122 Richard Feynman (1998) *The Meaning of It All: Thoughts of a Citizen Scientist*, Perseus. Feynman won the Nobel prize in Physics in 1965.

123 The renegade philosopher of science Paul Feyerabend argued precisely this point in relation to scientific discoveries in his book *Against Method* (Verso, 1975). Despite this title, Feyerabend wasn't denying the value of scientific

methods, he was arguing against hidebound adherence to any particular set of rules and methods. His anarchistic theory of knowledge argued for a more laissez-faire approach to combining multiple approaches, and being prepared to bend the rules when circumstances encouraged it. Feyerabend's work is controversial in science, which strives to articulate the objective truth that underpins events. But its spirit can less contentiously be applied to discovering the books, music, or films that you might find interesting. In these fields it is subjective opinions that count, not objective truth.

124 Entertainment Media Research and Olswang (2006) *Digital Music Survey*, www.entertainmentmediaresearch.com. In the US, terrestrial radio is reported to have its lowest number of listeners for several decades, but, according to data from Bridge Ratings, even there 45% of its survey sample said terrestrial radio was their preferred means of discovering music; curiously, television was not included in their responses ("Terrestrial radio still primary new music discovery destination," www.bridgeratings.com/press_07.21.06.New%20Music.htm).

125 Mark Thompson's Royal Television Society Fleming Lecture, "The BBC programmes and content in an on-demand world," 25 April 2006, www.bbc.co.uk/print/pressoffice/speeches/stories/thompson_fleming.shtml.

126 "Rivals round on BBC initiative," *The Guardian*, 25 April 2006, http://media.guardian.co.uk/broadcast/story/0,,1761193,00.html.

127 At the time of writing, Wikipedia (http://en.wikipedia.org/wiki/Crowdsourcing) cites the first use of this term as being Jeff Howe's in his June 2006 *Wired* article, "The rise of crowdsourcing," www.wired.com/wired/archive/14.06/crowds.html. Arguably, crowdsourcing has been in use since at least the nineteenth century when large numbers of volunteers contributed, by post, to help compile the first edition of the *Oxford English Dictionary*. It is also commonly cited as one of the success factors of open source software development.

128 "And now for some snuff comedy...," *The Guardian*, 24 October 2006, http://arts.guardian.co.uk/features/story/0,,1929884,00.html.

129 "You *do* like reading off a computer screen," *Locus Magazine*, March 2007, www.locusmag.com/Features/2007/03/cory-doctorow-you-do-like-reading-off.html (accessed 22 March 2007).

130 Examples include the Rhino Records "Rhinocast" (www.rhino.com/RZine/rhinocasts), Sub Pop Records (www.subpop.com/syndicate) and US music publisher BMI (www.bmi.com/podcast).

131 Cowboy Junkies official website at www.cowboyjunkies.com/exclusives/anatomy/anatomy.html.

132 For example: "Lily Allen – This year's girl," *The Independent*, 31 December 2006, http://enjoyment.independent.co.uk/music/features/article2114939.ece. For Hawthorne Heights, see "The hit factory," *Wired*, November 2005, www.wired.com/wired/archive/13.11/myspace.html.

133 "Music's new gatekeeper," *Wall Street Journal*, 9 March 2007, http://tinyurl.com/2eecsz (accessed 16 March 2007).

134 For details of this scenario, see, for example, Kusek & Leonhard, *op. cit.*; and William W. Fisher (2004) *Promises to Keep: Technology, Law, and the Future*

of Entertainment, Stanford University Press.

135 I say "may be able to" because when I started this chapter, several Norman McLaren films (including his Oscar-winning *Neighbours*) were available on YouTube, but were subsequently taken down, presumably at the request of copyright holders. A handful of other McLaren films then cropped up a few weeks later. Seven complete Bruce Conner films were available at the time of writing, plus one 'mashed up' with a new soundtrack.

136 This policy can be found at http://en.wikipedia.org/wiki/Wikipedia: Neutral_point_of_view.

137 Quoted in "Noel Gallagher attempts to start feud with overzealous record packagers," *Idolator* blog, 11 November 2006, www.idolator.com/ tunes/oasis/noel-gallagher-attempts-to-start-feud-with-overzealous-record-packagers-213323.php.

138 Coleman, *op. cit.* Sales increased from roughly $100 million in 1945 to $500 million in 1958 (I assume these figures are for the US market).

139 "No future," *The Guardian*, 6 January 2006, http://arts.guardian.co.uk/ harris/story/0,,1680003,00.html.

140 Heaney is quoted as saying that Eminem "has created a sense of what is possible. He has sent a voltage around a generation. He has done this not just through his subversive attitude but also his verbal energy." "Seamus Heaney praises Eminem," *BBC News Online*, 30 June 2003, http://news.bbc.co.uk/ 1/hi/entertainment/music/3033614.stm.

141 Boyd, *op. cit.*

142 "Web 'fuelling crisis in politics,'" *BBC News Online*, 17 November 2006, http://news.bbc.co.uk/1/hi/uk_politics/6155932.stm.

143 Malcolm Gladwell, "The Coolhunt," *The New Yorker*, 17 March 1997, www.gladwell.com/1997/1997_03_17_a_cool.htm.

Index